Sandra Alvarez

¡SABOR SABOR!
Sensational Spanish Flavors

Photography by Carin Verbruggen & Ferry Drenthem Soesman

TERRA

Preface

When I was asked to write the preface to Sandra's Spanish cookbook, I immediately said: 'Yes please!' During the competition of MasterChef Holland 2015 Sandra wholeheartedly defended her way of cooking with Spanish flavors. She cooks with passion and dedication and in my eyes, this is what defines a good chef.

What I remember most is Sandra defending her choice of preparing aioli without salt. Everybody who watched this program will remember this. Her recipes are very flavorful, but in the end, she did take some of our advice and added a pinch of salt to her dishes, even her aioli. Sandra's personality, combined with her creativity, her attention to healthy cooking and obviously her Spanish background are what make her so very special.

Get inspired by the recipes of this wonderful woman. Feel her love for Spanish cuisine and enjoy the dishes which were conceived in our MasterChef kitchen.

Michiel van der Eerde,
Judge on MasterChef Holland

Michiel is the chef/owner of restaurants Baut, Zuid and Restaurant C in Amsterdam and was elected the Most Outstanding Restaurant Entrepreneur of the Netherlands in 2017.

Contents

- Preface 2
- Introduction 6
- Indispensable for Spanish cooking 8
- Tapas and pinchos 17
- Soups 48
- Classics 63
- Healthy 114
- Happy Chic 140
- Holy aioli 165
- Sweets 181
- Cheers 208
- Overview of all recipes 216
- Index 218
- Acknowledgements 222

To Daniel, Rueben y Andrea

Introduction

Harry Mulisch, a famous Dutch author, once said that the soul travels on horseback. If that is the case, my soul is travelling somewhere between Santiago de Compostela and Ibiza and my soulless body is wandering the streets of Amsterdam.

My soul always wants to be in Spain. I was not born there but I am half Spanish and half Chinese. As a child, I spent every summer with my relatives in Spain, either in Santiago de Compostela or in Ibiza. These were endless summers during which I enjoyed life to the fullest with family and friends.

Every time I returned to the Netherlands, I missed the people but also the aromas and flavors of Spain. The smell of melting asphalt, the smell from the metro vents, the scent of Ducados cigarettes combined with Puig Agua Brava after-shave but above all the scent of pine trees and the taste of unrequited love, pan Bimbo and roasted garlic.

Maybe this longing is the reason I love to cook Spanish food. My soul is wandering around Spain. How can I long so much for a country even though I did not grow up there? Blame it on the blood. This is the source of my passion for everything Spanish.

I always want to feel, smell and taste Spain. Even during my MasterChef Holland adventure, I took every opportunity to prepare the flavors of Spain with love and passion.

I decided to write down and share my beloved Spanish recipes so that everyone, on any budget can prepare them. The tasteful photographs that accompany the recipes make even the most simple dish look like a masterpiece and will make you feel like you are in Spain.

These are classical Spanish dishes, but some have a surprising twist. In many recipes I tried to use less sugar, gave vegetables a more central role and added a vegetarian variation. The simple ingredients and easy to prepare recipes are typical of Spanish cuisine.

Join me on a culinary journey from Santiago de Compostela to Ibiza and get inspired to cook Spanish food.

Enjoy the flavors of Spain with **¡Sabor Sabor!**

Sandra

Indispensable for Spanish cooking

Invite the flavors of Spain into your pantry with these specialty ingredients:

- anise liqueur
- black garlic
- Brandy (Spanish Cognac)
- Cava (Spanish Champagne)
- chorizo
- extra virgin olive oil
  pure, cold-pressed olive oil; the best you can get. Spanish extra virgin olive oil is used in savory but also in sweet dishes.
- paella rice (short grain rice)
  the best paella rice is 'arroz bomba'; this is the king of rice because it absorbs a lot of liquid and therefore all the flavors of the stock in which it has been cooked.
- Manchego cheese
- Pedro Ximénez
  a sweet Sherry dessert wine, named for the Pedro Ximénez grape, also known as PX. It might be the sweetest wine in the world. Velvety and syrupy with the aromas of honey, dried fruits, coffee and dark chocolate, with just enough acidity to soften the extreme sweetness and the alcohol.
- pimentón
  smoked paprika which comes in two varieties, sweet and spicy. Its smoky aroma with earthy undertones gives any dish a Spanish touch. Pimentón de la Vera is the best brand since it is smoked very slowly.
- saffron
  a spice derived from the saffron crocus. It is used in savory and sweet dishes for its beautiful orange-yellow color but also for its rich warm flavor and aroma which is subtle and strong at the same time. Although it's not cheap, you only need a small quantity.
- Serrano ham or Iberian ham
- Sherry
- Sherry vinegar
  a strong vinegar with a nutty flavor made of the finest Sherry which has aged for 6 years. very good for vinaigrette, soups and sauces
- squid ink
- wine (red and white)

The following ingredients are not specific to Spanish cuisine, but I do use them for the recipes in this book:

- aniseed
- black pepper
- chickpeas (canned)
- cinnamon
- coarse sea salt or Maldon salt
- dark chocolate
- dried chili peppers
- eggs
- espelette pepper (Basque chili pepper)
- flat-leaf parsley (fresh)
- flour
- garlic
- garlic powder
- heavy cream
- honey
- bay leaves
- lemons
- milk
- onion
- oregano (dried or fresh)
- potatoes
- regular olive oil
- roasted peppers (from a jar)
- smoked salt
- smoked olive oil
- rosemary (dried or fresh)
- star anise
- Sichuan pepper
a spice named for the Sichuan province in China. Because of my Chinese roots, I like to add a little Chinese twist to my Spanish cooking. Sichuan pepper has a light citrusy flavor which goes very well with savory as well as sweet Spanish dishes. This 'pepper' is actually not a real pepper but belongs to Rutacae genus, the same plant family as citrus fruits. The peppercorns are actually the dried peels of tiny fruits. Sichuan pepper can give you a tingling feeling on your tongue and lips which makes for a very special eating sensation.
- sugar
- sunflower oil
- table salt
- thyme (dried or fresh)
- tomatoes
- tuna (canned)
- turmeric
- vanilla
- white lima beans (canned)
- white pepper

Kitchen tools:

Below is a list of the kitchen tools needed for the recipes in this book. Some of them are standard in any kitchen but probably not all of them. For this reason, I recommend that you read each recipe carefully to check which tools you will need.

- blender
- decorative toothpicks
- crème brûlée torch
- grill pan (with ridges)
- heavy (bottomed) skillet for sautéing
- immersion blender
- instant read thermometer
- melon baller
- (microplane) grater
- muffin/cupcake liners
- paella pan 30 cm/11 inches in diameter (after washing and drying, rub the pan with oil to prevent rust)
- paper towels
- parchment paper
- piping bag with a star tip
- plastic wrap
- sieve
- skillet or sauté pan
- soup pot
- Spanish style clay pot (ovenproof)
- springform pan with a 9 inch/22 cm diameter
- wooden skewers
- wooden spoons

Practical information:

Unless otherwise specified in the recipes, onions, garlic and potatoes should be peeled and vegetables should be washed before using.

¡Tapas y pinchos!
— Tapas and pinchos —

Tapas play a central role in Spanish culinary tradition. Their origin is the subject of many debates. What we do know is that tapas started out as slices of bread with olive oil, ham or cheese that were placed on top of Sherry glasses to preserve the flavor and keep out flying insects. The slices of bread covering the glasses were called *tapas*, Spanish for covers. This was the humble beginning of a Spanish treat that has become immensely popular all over the world.

Nowadays tapas are made with many different ingredients and have become little pieces of art. They can be served warm or cold, as a snack, an appetizer or as a main course. Like many other Spanish dishes, tapas are great for sharing.

When you eat tapas, it is not just about the food but also about the company. Eating tapas brings people together because you share the food. It is a completely different experience from just eating one dish from your own plate.

I love to prepare and serve tapas when I have not seen my friends or family for a long time and we have a lot of catching up to do. These little dishes symbolize joy and the good life. Whether it is at home or at a restaurant, when you eat tapas, you are guaranteed a long, enjoyable evening at the dinner table. In a tapas bar, these delicacies are displayed on the counter in a way that makes it hard to resist the temptation. You might as well give in and enjoy the experience.

A *pincho* or *pintxo* in Basque is a traditional Basque snack that is 'pinned down' on a slice of bread with a skewer or decorative toothpick. The Spanish verb *pinchar* means 'to pin'.

Tapas and pinchos seem very similar, but how they differ is also the subject of debate. What they have in common is that they both consist of small portions. Among my Spanish family and friends, the rule is: if you need cutlery to eat it, it is a tapa. A pincho is always smaller and has the telltale skewer or toothpick.

Pincho de champiñones - Mushroom pinchos

Makes 6

- 12 large mushrooms
- ½ onion
- 2 garlic cloves
- 4 tbsp olive oil (plus a little extra for drizzling)
- ½ tbsp butter
- ¼ tsp anise seeds (powdered or whole)
- 2 tbsp Pedro Ximénez wine or Sherry
- 1 tsp honey
- flat-leaf parsley
- 18 large shrimp, peeled
- 6 baguette slices
- 6 skewers/decorative toothpicks

Cut the stems off the mushrooms and chop these into small pieces. Finely chop the onion and garlic. Heat the olive oil and butter in a heavy skillet and sauté the onion and garlic for a few minutes over medium-high heat. Add the whole mushrooms, the chopped stems and the anise seed. Turn up the heat and sauté the mixture for about 2 more minutes.

Add the Pedro Ximénez and honey and sauté for an additional 5 minutes until the mushrooms are tender and golden. Finely chop the parsley and add to the mushroom mixture. Remove the mixture from the pan and sauté the shrimp in the remaining butter and oil for about 2 minutes over medium-high heat. Toast the baguette slices and drizzle some olive oil on top. Separate the whole mushrooms from the mushroom mixture. Spread the mixture over 6 baguette slices. Place 2 whole mushrooms on each slice and 3 shrimp on top of this, securing each little tower with a skewer.

Variations:
- Instead of shrimp you can also use a slice of Manchego cheese.

Pincho de dátil relleno y jamón Serrano - Stuffed dates and Serrano ham pinchos

Makes 18

- 18 pitted dates
- 9 tsp orange marmalade or fig jam
- 18 almonds
- 18 slices of Serrano ham
- 18 arugula leaves (more if small)
- 4 tbsp olive oil
- 18 skewers/decorative toothpicks

Stuff each date with ½ teaspoon marmalade or fig jam and one almond. Spread out the Serrano ham and place one or more arugula leaves on top. Place a date on each slice of ham and arugula and roll up tightly. Secure the rolls with a skewer. Heat the olive oil in a frying pan and sauté the rolls for 1 to 2 minutes until crispy. Let the rolls drain on a paper towel.

Pincho con plátano y jamón Serrano - Banana and Serrano ham pinchos

Makes 12

- 3 large bananas
- 12 slices of Serrano ham
- olive oil
- 12 skewers/decorative toothpicks

Peel the bananas and cut each of them into 4 pieces. Wrap each piece of banana with a slice of Serrano ham and secure with a skewer. Heat the olive oil in a frying pan and sauté the rolls a few minutes over medium heat until golden on all sides.

Higos asados con jamon ibérico and queso de cabra - Grilled figs with Iberian ham and goat cheese

Makes 6

- 6 walnuts
- 6 fresh figs
- 2 tbsp honey
- 1 tsp chopped fresh rosemary
- 6 tbsp fresh goat cheese
- 6 large slices Iberian ham
- coarse sea salt or Maldon sea salt

Preheat the oven to 350 °F/180 °C. Chop the walnuts. Cut the tips off the figs and cut crosswise making sure the bottom stays in one piece. Mix the nuts, honey, rosemary and salt with the goat cheese. Stuff the figs with the goat cheese mixture. Wrap the Iberian ham around the figs. Secure with a skewer. Arrange the rolls on a baking sheet lined with parchment paper. Broil for 7-8 minutes. Remove from the oven and allow to rest for a few minutes. Serve lukewarm.

🍷 A young red Tempranillo or Spanish beer.

¡Bomba de la Barceloneta!
— Potato-meatball Barceloneta style —

Ground beef/pork and mashed potatoes are the main ingredients for this famous tapa from Barceloneta, one of Barcelona's seaside neighborhoods. This Flavour Bomb is a simple combination that succeeds in blending the taste and the texture of meatballs and mashed potatoes inside a crispy shell

Eat this tapa with a spicy salsa brava and aioli and you will love it as much as I do. The name of the dish is a reference to the bombardment of Barceloneta during the Civil War and is an homage to those who died.

Makes 6

- 1 lb/450 g Russet potatoes or other starchy potato
- salt
- 3 tbsp olive oil
- 3 eggs
- black pepper and/or cayenne pepper
- ¼ lb/125 g ground beef
- ¼ lb/125 g ground pork
- 1 onion
- 1 tomato
- 1 tbsp Pedro Ximénez wine or Sherry
- ½ cup/100 g breadcrumbs
- Iberian salt (see recipe on page 174) or pimentón (smoked paprika)
- 2 cups/½ liter olive oil for frying
- aioli (see recipe on page 166) or aioli with Sichuan pepper (see recipe on page 166)
- salsa brava (see recipe on page 68)

Boil the unpeeled potatoes with a pinch of salt for about 30-45 minutes. Puree them with a fork or a masher adding 3 tbsp of olive oil and one whole egg. Season with salt and pepper.

While the potatoes are boiling, mix the ground pork and ground beef and season with salt and pepper. Dice the onion. Grate the tomato. Finely chop the garlic. Heat 2 tbsp of olive oil in a heavy skillet and sauté the onion with a pinch of salt for about 3 minutes over medium heat. Add the garlic and the ground meat and sauté for about 10 minutes until the meat is golden brown and crispy. The meat should be stirred as you brown so the pieces are as small as possible. Add the tomato and let it simmer for another 2 minutes. Add the Pedro Ximénez wine and cook for another minute until the wine has evaporated. Let it cool.

Beat the remaining eggs in a deep dish. In a separate dish, mix the breadcrumbs with a pinch of Iberian salt and/or smoked paprika. Mix the ground meat with the mashed potatoes. Take some breadcrumbs in your hand and shape the potato/meat mixture into balls that are slightly smaller than a tennis ball. Dip the balls into the egg dish and then roll them in the breadcrumbs.

Heat the olive oil (350 °F/180 °C) in a deep frying pan or fryer and fry the balls for about 2 min per side over high heat until golden brown and crispy. While frying, three quarters of the balls should be covered by the oil. Let the balls drain on a paper towel.

Serve with 1 tbsp aioli and 2 tbsp salsa brava for each bomba.

Variation: Add some diced chili pepper to the meat for an extra kick.

🍷 A typical wine from the Northeast of Spain, such as a Somontano.

¡Pan de tinta de calamar!
— Bread with squid ink —

The special ingredient for this mysterious black bread is squid ink. When I am cooking a Spanish dinner for family or friends, I always prepare this bread and everyone loves it. The flavor is surprisingly mild and subtle and the deep color is a sight to behold.

Serves 8

1 ¼ cup/300 ml whole milk
6 packets of squid ink (4 g each)
1 packet dry yeast (7g)
1 tsp salt
1 tsp sugar or honey
4 cups/500 g all-purpose flour

Heat the milk over low heat (do not let it boil) and add the ink. Mix well. Remove from heat and first add the yeast followed by the salt and the sugar or honey.
Bit by bit add the flour and knead the dough for a few minutes until smooth and elastic. Let the dough rise for 1-2 hours in a warm, dry place until it has doubled in size. Preheat the oven to 400°F/200°C. Knead the dough for a few minutes to release the air. Grease a baking tin and bake the bread for 25-30 minutes until done.

A dry Rueda Verdejo.

¡Buñuelos de bacalao!
— Salted cod fritters —

Maria Antonia was a seamstress who used to come to my Spanish grandmother's house once a week to mend clothes. This was customary in my family in those days. Every summer Maria Antonia would take my measurements and make me a smocked dress, a classic embroidered dress that I was not ever going to wear to high school in Amsterdam.
Because the dress was a present, I accepted the gift every year.

Maria Antonia had a special scent. 'She smells like cod' is what I was told, 'because she wears a corset'. Not knowing what a corset was, this explanation was a complete mystery to me, but it did keep me from eating codfish for years. Half a century later, I spotted something with 'bacalao' on the menu of a restaurant in Barcelona. I decided to order what turned out to be a type of fritter served with 'miel de caña' (molasses). Maria Antonia's corset was instantly wiped from my memory.

Serves 4

5 oz/150 g salted cod
1 garlic clove
3 spring onions
1 tbsp flat-leaf parsley
1 egg
½ tsp dry yeast
2/3 cup/ 75 g all-purpose flour
2/3 cup/150 ml lukewarm water
olive oil

Soak the salted cod according to the instructions on the packaging. This process can take hours. Rinse the fish under running water. Puree the fish with the garlic, the spring onions and the parsley in a food processor. Beat the egg and mix it into the fish with a fork. Combine the flour, the yeast and the water in a bowl and mix into a batter. Bit by bit, spoon the batter into the cod mixture and stir until creamy. Let this rest for a few minutes. In the meantime, heat a generous amount of olive oil in a frying pan. (The fritters should be covered while frying). Test the temperature of the oil by tossing in a bit of bread. When it instantly turns golden brown, the oil is at the right temperature. Take one tablespoon batter at the time and fry the fritters for about 2 minutes on each side over medium-high heat until they puff up and are golden brown and crunchy. Let them drain on paper towel.

Serving suggestion: Drizzle with molasses, honey or aioli with saffron (see recipe on page 166)

🍷 A dry Rueda Verdejo.

¡Croquetas cremosas españolas!
— Creamy Spanish croquettes —

The croquette was invented by one of the chefs of King Louis XIV. This dish became popular all over the world including Spain, where you can find it in almost any tapas bar. Spanish croquettes have a soft, creamy bechamel filling which melts in your mouth. They are usually round or oval and not too big. A perfect tapa!

When I was little, we used to have a whole leg of Serrano ham sitting on the kitchen counter. This big ham definitely spiced up our suburban kitchen.

The croquettes we used to make at home were delicious because of the bechamel sauce. My father would saw off a bit of the ham bone and we would add this to the milk while it was cooking. The bechamel sauce would have this wonderful, intense ham flavor. More like an explosion of flavors in your mouth which no store-bought sauce could ever top.

It's not hard to make Spanish croquettes, if you are not in a hurry.

I usually prepare many different varieties at a time and freeze the extras to surprise unexpected guests. Homemade croquettes are always a big hit at my house.

Makes 10

- Croquetas de jamón ibérico o serrano -
- ¼ cup/30 g onion
- 2 tbsp/30 g butter
- 3–4 oz/80–100 g Iberian or Serrano ham
- 1¼ cup/ 300 ml whole milk
- ¼ cup/30 g all-purpose flour (for the bechamel)
- salt
- black pepper
- nutmeg
- 1 cup/130 g all-purpose flour (for the crust)
- 1 cup/150 g breadcrumbs
- 1 egg
- 1¼ cup/300 ml olive oil

Chop the onion finely and sauté for about 4 minutes in butter over a medium-high heat until translucent. Cut the ham into small pieces, add to the pan and sauté for another minute. Heat the milk until it is lukewarm and set aside.

Croquetas de jamón ibérico o serrano - Iberian or Serrano ham croquettes
Add the flour to the pan with onion and ham and stir with a wooden spoon for 3–4 minutes over medium-high heat until a paste forms which separates from the pan and just starts to brown. Pour in the lukewarm milk bit by bit while stirring continuously. Wait each time until the milk has been absorbed before adding more. During this process the bechamel should cook slowly over medium-high heat. After about 5 minutes the bechamel should thicken. Using your wooden spoon, make a line through the middle of the bechamel, if this flows back slowly, it is thick enough.

Season with salt, pepper and a pinch of nutmeg. Do not over-salt, remember the ham is salty. Pour the bechamel in large dish, cover with foil and let it set in the refrigerator for at least two hours. Once it is set, cut the bechamel into 10 pieces of equal size. Pour the flour and the breadcrumbs into two separate, shallow bowls. Beat the egg. Rub some olive oil on your hands and shape the bechamel into oval croquettes. Roll these in the flour, then dip them in the egg and finally coat them with the breadcrumbs. Heat the olive oil in a deep frying pan until it reaches a temperature of 350°F/180°C and fry the croquettes, 5 at a time, for about 3 minutes over medium-high heat until golden brown. (Test the temperature of the oil by tossing in a bit of bread. When it instantly turns golden brown, the oil is at the right temperature.)

Serving suggestion: Delicious with aioli. (see recipe on page 166)

Variation to add extra flavor to the bechamel: Bring the milk to a boil with 1 fl. oz of heavy cream and add a piece of Serrano ham bone. Cover and cook over low heat for about 20 minutes.

- Croquetas de gambas -
3–4 oz/80–90 g (frozen) shrimp
½ garlic clove
1¼ cup/ 300 ml whole milk
1 fl oz/30 ml olive oil
¼ cup/30 g all-purpose flour
salt
white pepper
nutmeg
1 cup/130 g all-purpose flour
1 cup/150 g breadcrumbs
1 egg
1¼ cup/300 ml olive oil

- Croquetas vegetarianas -
3 oz/80 g kale or spinach
3 oz/80 g Manchego cheese
1¼ cup/ 300 ml whole milk
2 tbsp/30 g butter
salt
black pepper
nutmeg
1 cup/130 g all-purpose flour
(for the crust)
1 cups/150 g breadcrumbs
1 egg
1¼ cup/300 ml olive oil

Croquetas de gambas - shrimp croquettes
If needed, defrost the shrimp and chop finely. Crush the garlic. Heat the olive oil in a skillet and sauté the shrimp with the garlic, salt and pepper for about 1–2 minutes over medium-high heat. Continue to prepare just like the ham croquettes.

Serving suggestion: Serve with squid ink aioli or orange and honey aioli (recipes on page 166)

Variation: Add a few drops of smoked olive oil and a packet of squid ink to the bechamel.

Croquetas vegetarianas - vegetarian croquettes
Finely chop the kale or spinach. Grate the Manchego cheese. Heat the milk and keep it lukewarm. Heat the butter in a skillet and sauté the kale or spinach (with a pinch of salt and pepper) for 5 minutes over low to medium-high heat. Continue to prepare as the ham croquettes but add the Manchego cheese once the bechamel is done.

Serving suggestion: Delicious with aioli and pear (see recipe on page 166)

Variations:
-Substitute the kale or spinach with ¼ cup chopped onions.
-Try to make round croquettes instead of oval ones.

🍷 A young red Tempranillo or a Spanish beer.

¡Tapa de endivias con cabrales y nueces!
— Cabrales cheese and walnuts —

I think I have had this tapa at every wedding I have ever attended. It is a very beautiful dish. The endives resemble spoons and therefore make a great base for tapas. In Spain this tapa is often made with Cabrales, a blue cheese from the town of Cabrales near the Picos de Europa National Park in northwestern Spain. This cheese can only be made with milk from this area. The interesting thing about this cheese, is that it can be made not only with milk from cows but also with milk from goats and/or sheep. The variety made with cow's milk is creamier while that made with goat and/or sheep milk gives the cheese a stronger flavor. The cheeses are ripened in the natural caves of Cabrales where it is cool and humid. Since Cabrales is not available everywhere, Roquefort is a good alternative.

Serves 4

2 white or red endives
1 tbsp/10 g butter
¼ cup/50 ml milk
2/3 cup/150 ml heavy cream
½ cup/50g Cabrales or Roquefort cheese
1 tsp corn starch
salt
black pepper
¾ cup/100 g walnuts

Trim the base of the endives and separate the leaves. Rinse and dry with a paper towel. Heat the butter in a saucepan and add the milk and cream, stirring regularly. Remove from heat right before it starts to boil. Add the cheese and the cornstarch. Put the pan back on the stove and heat over low heat and stir for a few minutes until the sauce thickens. Season with a pinch of salt and pepper. Let the sauce cool off. Chop half of the walnuts and stir them into the cheese mixture. Divide the cheese mixture over the individual endive leaves and then top each one with a walnut half.

🍷 A full bodied red wine such as a Priorat or a Syrah blend from the Terra Alta region.

¡Queso Manchego en aceite de oliva!
— Manchego cheese marinated in olive oil —

Manchego is a cheese made in the La Mancha region of Spain from the milk of the sheep of the Manchega breed. The name 'Manchego" has a protected status (P.O.D. Protected Designation of Origin) provided the cheese has aged for more than two months.

Manchego cheese comes in several varieties, *tierno* (young), *semicurado* (semi-cured), *curado* (cured) and *viejo* (aged). Marinating Manchego cheese in olive oil has been a traditional means of preservation for Spanish cheese farmers for centuries. Adding garlic and herbs to the oil gives the cheese a truly wonderful flavor. Try this oil-cured cheese with a piece of crunchy bread, *pan con tomate* (see recipe on page 38) or just by itself.

Serves 4

5 oz/150 g (young) Manchego cheese
1 bay leaf
1 sprig fresh rosemary
¼ tbsp peppercorns (black, pink or mixed)
1 garlic clove
extra virgin olive oil

Cut the Manchego into triangles about 3 inches long and 0.2 inch thick. Put the triangles in a sealable glass jar with the bay leaf, rosemary, peppercorns and garlic. Pour in sufficient oil until all the cheese is covered. Seal the jar and place it in the refrigerator. After a few days the herbs and garlic have infused the cheese with a delicious aroma. Serve at room temperature.

Serving suggestion: Sprinkle the cheese with some freshly ground coffee.

Variation:
-add a few drops of smoked olive oil to the marinade or use smoked or black garlic.
-add ¼ tsp Sichuan peppercorns

🍷 A full-bodied red wine such as a Priorat.

¡Chips de berenjenas con miel!
— Eggplant chips with honey —

Once you have tried these, chances are you will never want to eat store bought chips again. This is a very popular tapa which is easy to prepare and surprisingly good. In Spain it is served with *miel de caña* (molasses) but it is just as delicious with honey. It might seem surprising to dip the chips in water before frying them in hot oil but this way you rinse off the excess flour. I have seen my family in Spain do this many a time.

Serves 4

2 eggplants
1 tsp salt
1¼ cup/300 ml olive oil
2/3 cup/75 g all-purpose flour
2 cups/500 ml lukewarm water
coarse sea salt
½ cup/150 g honey

-Rosemary Salt-
1 tbsp coarse sea salt
1 tbsp fresh rosemary

Cut the eggplants into thin slices. Sprinkle salt on both sides and let them 'sweat' for 30–60 minutes. This way the slices will not absorb too much oil while frying. Pat dry with a paper towel. Heat the olive oil to 350°F/180°C in a heavy skillet. Take the eggplant slices, first dip them in the flour and then in the lukewarm water. Fry the slices 2–3 minutes on each side until they are golden brown. Let the slices dry on paper towel. Sprinkle with sea salt. Finish with a drizzle of honey.

Grind the sea salt and rosemary with a mortar and pestle.

Variation: Sprinkle a pinch of rosemary salt and/or cinnamon over the eggplant chips.

🍷 These chips go very well with a glass of Cava, a beer or any good Spanish wine.

¡Pan con tomate!
— Catalan tomato bread —

There are a lot of stories about the origins of this recipe, among others that it was invented to mask the taste of low-quality ham from Catalonia.
Whatever its origins, *pan con tomate* has become a much-loved tapa or side dish which tastes great with a glass of wine or a beer. Surprisingly, it also goes well with coffee which makes it a popular breakfast choice.

You can serve pan con tomate with many different Spanish delicacies. The options are endless for carnivores and vegetarians. Mix and match. Be creative!

Grilled bread, tomato, garlic, olive oil and salt. Pure perfection as far as I am concerned.

Makes 8

2 ripe tomatoes
2 garlic cloves
8 slices of firm bread such as sourdough, another artisan bread, or a baguette
extra virgin olive oil
coarse sea salt

Makes 4

- Pan con tomate con manchego -
4 slices of pan con tomate
1-2 tbsp pepper jelly (recipe on page 172)
4 slices Manchego cheese
honey for drizzling
4 chopped walnuts

- Pan con tomate con jamón serrano o ibérico -
pan con tomate
Serrano or Iberian ham
extra virgin olive oil

- Pan con tomate vegetal -
pan con tomate
pepper jelly or tomato jam (recipe on page 172 and 45)
red bell peppers escalivada (see recipe on page 74)
olive oil
coarse sea salt

Pan con tomate
Halve the tomatoes and the garlic cloves. Grill the bread under the broiler or toast in in the toaster until crunchy and golden brown. Rub the garlic on the bread. Rub the inside of the tomato on the bread, allowing the juice to soak in. Drizzle with olive oil and sprinkle with salt. Serve at once before the bread turns soggy.

Pan con tomate con manchego - Pan con tomate with Manchego cheese
Spread a layer of pepper jelly on the pan con tomate. Add a few slices of Manchego cheese. Drizzle with honey. Sprinkle with the walnuts. Heat under the broiler for a few minutes until the cheese is melted.

Variation: Substitute the pepper jelly with either tomato jam (recipe on page 45), sobrasada vegana (see recipe on page 44) or any aioli (recipes on page 166)

Pan con tomate con jamón serrano o Ibérico - Pan con tomate with Serrano or Iberian ham

Place a few slices of Serrano or Iberian ham on the *pan con tomate*. Drizzle with olive oil.

Variation: Spread some aioli (see recipes on page 166) on the *pan con tomate* before adding the ham. Sprinkle some grated Manchego cheese on top of the ham.

Pan con tomate vegetal - vegetarian pan con tomate
Spread some pepper jelly or tomato jelly on the pan con tomate. Place some strips of roasted bell peppers on top, drizzle with olive oil and season with salt.

Variation: Use roasted peppers from a jar and garnish with a Padron pepper.

Pan con tomate is also a great base for pinchos (see recipes on page 17). You can make these pinchos any size you like, small, large or even very tall. You secure them with a skewer or a decorative toothpick as they do in many tapas bars.

Pincho suggestions: combine the pan con tomate with:
-Tortilla de patatas (see recipe on page 63) and a Padron pepper (see recipe on page 70)
-Pulpo on any kind of mash (see recipes on page 158)
-Oxtail in chocolate wine sauce (see recipe on page 90)
-Ensaladilla rusa vegetal (see recipe on page 72)

🍷 A young red Tempranillo such as a Rioja or a Catalonian red wine.

¡Tabla de delicias ibéricas!
— Spanish Cheese and Charcuterie platter —

According to lore, even the Spanish kings of the 13th and 15th centuries, Alfonso X and Fernando II, used to cap their drinks with a slice of bread with cheese or ham to keep insects away. Little did they know that these caps, or *tapas* in Spanish, would grow from their humble beginnings into a culinary rage many centuries later. They could have never imagined that these tapas would become the showcase of Spanish cuisine all over the world.

Below are some of my favorite Spanish cheeses and cured meats with some breads and spreads. Serve these tapas on a large platter or a wooden board. Just pick and choose and get in a Spanish mood together with your loved ones.

Spanish Cheeses

Manchego – a hard sheep cheese, from Castile-La Mancha.

Cabrales – a strong, rich, blue cheese made from sheep, goat or cow milk from Asturias.

Idiazabal – a smoked hard cheese made from unpasteurized sheep milk.

Mahón – a medium hard cheese with bit of a tangy flavor, made from cow milk, from the island of Menorca.

Tetilla – a medium hard cheese, mild and buttery, made from cow milk, from Galicia.

Roncal – a lightly smoked hard sheep-milk cheese, from Navarre.

Membrillo or dulce de membrillo ¬– quince jelly, often served with Manchego cheese.

Spanish cured meats

Chorizo – a spicy hard sausage (fresh, dried or smoked) made from pork and 'pimiento choricero', a special type of bell pepper.

Fuet – a skinny salami with a sweet, mild flavor, from Catalonia.

Serrano ham – a mild, dry-cured ham with a warm flavor, made from the meat of white pigs fed on corn and grain.

Iberian ham or *pata negra* – a melt-in-your-mouth ham, made from the meat of the black Iberian pig. These pigs primarily feed on herbs, berries and acorns which gives this ham a unique flavor. The fat of this ham is mainly unsaturated, therefore similar to olive oil.

Cecina – a salt-cured, air-dried beef, nicely marbled with a mellow, buttery flavor.

Lomo – a sausage made from the lean, air-cured pork loin of a white pig.

Breads and spreads:

Pan Payés – peasant bread (recipe on page 78)

Picos – breadsticks, fried in olive oil

Boquerones en aceite de oliva – anchovies in olive oil.

Aceitunas aliñadas con limón, ajo y hinojo - marinated olives with lemon, garlic and fennel

Wash the lemon and cut into small pieces. Halve the garlic cloves and remove the germ to avoid a bitter flavor. Chop the fennel greens. Pour the olive oil in a glass jar, add the olives, lemon, garlic and fennel greens. Put the jar in the refrigerator and leave it there for a few days, shaking the jar every now and then. The olives will absorb all the other flavors. You can keep them in the refrigerator for a week but, in my experience, they will disappear as soon as you serve them.

Serves 4

-Aceitunas aliñadas-
½ lemon
2 garlic cloves
3 sprigs of fennel greens
10 oz/300 g mixed olives
1/3 cup/70 ml olive oil

Sobrasada vegana - vegan spread (chorizo flavor)
Sobrasada is a raw, spreadable sausage from the Balearic Islands made with ground pork, smoked paprika and other spices. The flavor is very similar to chorizo. In Spain it's available everywhere, in stores as well as restaurants. Whenever I get the chance, I indulge myself, especially when it's freshly prepared. Once I start eating it, I can't stop. But in all honesty, it's not a very healthy thing to eat. For this reason, I came up with this vegan version which you can enjoy without the guilt.

Drain and chop the sundried tomatoes. Mince the garlic and chop the almonds or pine nuts.
Mix the tomatoes, garlic, nuts, parsley, with all the spices and the olive oil. Puree until smooth and season with salt and pepper.

Serves 8

-Sobrasada vegana-
1 ½ cup/150 g sundried tomatoes in oil
1 garlic clove
½ cup/50 g roasted almonds or pine nuts
1 tbsp flat-leaf parsley
2 tsp smoked paprika
1 tbsp fresh parsley
1 tsp powdered cumin
¼ tsp aniseed
½ tsp oregano
½ cup/100 ml olive oil
salt
black pepper

Tostada con sobrasada vegana, miel y almendras - Toasted bread with vegan sobrasada, honey and almonds
Preheat the oven to 350°F/180°C. Chop the almonds. Toast the bread and drizzle with olive oil. Mix the honey into the sobrasada and spread this mixture on the bread. Sprinkle the chopped almonds on top. Place the bread in the oven until the almonds turn golden brown.

Variation for carnivores – Substitute the vegan sobrasada with the 'authentic' sobrasada. (available at a Spanish specialty store or online).

Serves 2

-Tostada con sobrasada vegana-
1 tbsp chopped almonds
2 slices of firm bread, such as sourdough or baguette
5 tbsp sobrasada vegana
1 tbsp honey
1 tbsp olive oil

Makes 4 jars (1 cup/250 ml)

-Dulce de tomate-
2 lbs/1 kg ripe tomatoes
2 cups/500 g dark brown sugar
1 cinnamon stick

Optional
1 star anise pod

Dulce de tomate - tomato jam
Bring a pot of water to a boil. Score the tomatoes and place them in the boiling water for a few minutes. Peel and chop finely. Transfer the tomatoes to a sauce pan, add the sugar and mix well. Cover the pan and cook for about 90 minutes over low heat until all the juice from the tomatoes has been reduced and the jam has reached the desired thickness. Add the cinnamon stick and the star anise (optional) after 30 minutes.
Remove the cinnamon stick (and the star anise) and divide the jam over the glass jars. Store in the refrigerator. The tomato jam keeps for months.

Suggestion: A jar of tomato jam makes a very nice present.

Serves 4

-Paté de almendras y aceitunas-
1 ½ cup/150 g peeled almonds
1/2 cup/100 g pitted olives
1 garlic clove
3 tbsp/50 ml olive oil
3 tbsp/50 ml Pedro Ximénez or Sherry
salt
black pepper

Paté de almendras y aceitunas - Almond-olive spread
Roast the almonds until golden brown and place them in a blender. Add the olives, garlic, the olive oil, Pedro Ximénez or Sherry. Puree and season with salt and pepper. This spread keeps for a few days in the refrigerator.

Serving suggestion: Toast a piece of bread, drizzle with olive oil, add a layer of the almond-olive spread, sprinkle with Espellete pepper (Basque chili pepper) and top with a slice of Manchego and a slice of pear.

Serves 4–6

-Mahonesa de moras-
1/3 cup/90 ml good quality red wine
3 oz/80 g (frozen) blackberries
or 1 tsp blackberry jam
¼ tsp thyme
a few (pink) peppercorns
5 tbsp mayonnaise

Makes 3,5 oz/100 g

-Crema de aceitunas-
1/2 cup/100 ml heavy cream
10 pitted green olives
10 tbsp lemon juice
salt
black pepper

Mahonesa de moras - blackberry mayonnaise
A spectacular creamy mayonnaise which is delicious with red meat or game but also with fries. Heat the red wine with the blackberries in a sauce pan. Boil until reduced by half. Allow to cool and mix with the mayonnaise. Store in the refrigerator.

Crema de aceitunas - olive spread
Place all the ingredients in a blender and puree until smooth. This spread keeps for a few days in the refrigerator.

🍷 With the platter, a robust red wine such as a Priorat or a Ribera del Duero Crianza.

¡Ajoblanco!
— Almond gazpacho —

Ajoblanco, the pale sister of gazpacho, is a cold soup from Andalucía. It has a creamy texture but is also surprisingly refreshing. It is delicious on a hot summer day and easy to prepare. When I long for Spain and sunshine, I prepare this soup. Even in wintertime. When I feel a cold coming on, a shot of ajoblanco will perk me right up. You can make this soup as thick or garlicky as you like by changing the proportions of the ingredients. This version is my personal favorite.

Serves 4–8

- 2 cups/500 ml water
- 2 slices/50 g white bread without crust
- 1 cup/150 g white almonds
- 1 garlic clove
- 1–2 tsp Sherry vinegar
- ¼ tsp salt
- ½ melon
- about 25 seedless grapes
- ¼ to 1/3 cup/25–50 ml olive oil
- black pepper

Optional: ½ tsp vinegar

Soak the bread with the almonds and the garlic in 1 cup of water until it softens. Add the Sherry vinegar and the salt. Use a melon spoon to make melon balls and halve the grapes. Puree the bread mixture and pour in the olive oil bit by bit. Start with 1 fl oz of olive oil, you can always add more later. Slowly pour in the other cup of water until the soup has the consistency of heavy cream. If needed, add some more water. If it is too liquid, add another piece of bread and puree again. Season with salt and pepper and (optional) ½ teaspoon of vinegar. If you prefer a finer texture, pass the soup through a sieve. Refrigerate for at least two hours before serving.

Serving suggestion: Place a few melon balls and grapes on the bottom of a deep plate or glass. Pour in the ajoblanco and drizzle with extra virgin olive oil.

Variation: Add some radish slices and/or fresh mint leaves.

🍷 A dry Rioja Rosado (Spanish rosé) or a dry Sherry.

¡Sopa de pescado vasca!
— Basque fish soup —

My honeymoon was a road trip across Spain. We drove straight from Holland to Irún, a small town close to San Sebastián. We arrived around midnight at a small inn. The restaurant next door was still open and they were prepared to heat up some fish soup. The soup had one remarkable ingredient, a special kind of bread with a thick black crust (*sopako/pan de pistola*). I have never had such a wonderful soup again. You could just taste the sea. I would love to get married again and honeymoon in the Basque country just to have this soup one more time.

Serves 4–6

-Fish stock-
flat-leaf parsley
1 lb/500 g of fish heads, tails and bones of any kind of white fish such as hake, mullet, cod or monkfish
6 cups/1 ½ l water
salt

-Base-
4 slices/100 g bread (ciabatta or some other firm white bread)
1 onion
1 carrot
2 leeks
2 garlic cloves
2–3 ripe tomatoes
3 tbsp olive oil
salt
½–1 tsp smoked paprika
¼ cup/50 ml Spanish Brandy or Cognac
¾ cup/150 ml white wine
white pepper

-Garnish-
1 lb/500 g white fish filets such as hake, mullet, cod or monkfish
salt
all-purpose flour
2–3 tbsp olive oil
1 lb/500 g shrimp
½ lb/250 g of clams

Optional: smoked paprika oil (see recipe on page 168)

Finely cut the parsley. Boil the fish heads, tails and bones for about 20 minutes in the water with a large pinch of salt. Every now and then remove the foam. Pass the stock through a sieve and set aside.

If you don't have time to prepare your own stock, you can buy some from the fish counter at your local deli or grocery store.

Roast the bread for about 3 minutes in the toaster or oven until golden. Finely chop all the vegetables and the garlic. Heat the olive oil in a heavy-bottomed soup pot and sauté the onions, carrots and leeks, with the garlic and a pinch of salt, for about 5 minutes over medium-high heat. Add the tomatoes and smoked paprika and stir well. Sauté for another 5 minutes. Cut the bread into small pieces and add to the pan. Sauté the mixture over low heat for 1–2 minutes. Add the Brandy or Cognac and let it reduce.
Add white wine and let it reduce again for a few minutes. Add the fish stock and let it cook for 20 minutes. Puree the soup and season with salt and white pepper.

Cut the fish into pieces and sprinkle with salt. Roll the fish in the flour. Heat the olive oil in a heavy skillet and sauté the shrimp for a few minutes over high heat. Pour in some more olive oil and add the clams. After the clams open, add the fish and sauté for another 1–2 minutes over medium-high heat. Place the fish, the shrimp and the clams in a deep plate and pour in the fish soup.

Optional: Drizzle with smoked paprika oil.

🍷 A dry white wine from northern Spain.

¡Fabada vegetal!
— Vegetarian bean stew —

This vegetarian white bean soup was inspired by the *Fabada Asturiana*. The name comes from the Asturian *faves*, or beans. A traditional fabada is made with different kinds of pork, cured ham, chorizo, bacon and blood sausage. The smoked paprika adds the smoky aroma and the deep red color which makes for a lovely contrast with the white beans. My grandmother was from Asturias and she might roll over in her grave if she found out that I made a version of her signature dish without meat. The traditional fabada is made with large, dried, white lima beans (also known as butter beans) which should be soaked overnight. For this recipe I used large canned lima beans.

Serves 4

1 carrot
1 (red) onion
3 garlic cloves
1 small red bell pepper
1 small green bell pepper
olive oil
5 saffron threads
2 tbsp oregano
¼ tsp cumin
½ tsp cinnamon
salt
black pepper
2 tsp smoked paprika
2 cans (15 oz/425 g) large lima/butter beans
1½ cup/350 ml water
1 bay leaf
9 oz/250 g mixed mushrooms
1 garlic clove
1 tsp smoked paprika

Optional: Iberian salt
(see recipe on page 174)

Grate the carrot. Finely chop the onion and garlic. Remove the seeds from the bell peppers and cut into strips. Heat 4 tbsp of olive oil in a (heavy-bottomed) soup pot and add the carrot, onion, garlic, peppers, saffron, oregano, cumin, cinnamon and a pinch of salt and pepper. Sauté over medium-high heat for about 5 minutes. Add 2 tsp smoked paprika at the last minute but be careful that it doesn't burn.

Puree 1 cup of the beans with ¼ cup of water and drain the rest of the beans. Add 1 cup of water and the bay leaf to the vegetables together with the pureed beans and cook for about 10 minutes over low heat. Taste to see if it needs more salt.

Chop the mushrooms into large chunks. Heat 4 tbsp olive oil in a heavy skillet and sauté the mushrooms with the crushed garlic clove for 5 minutes. The mushrooms should still be a bit al dente. Add 1 tsp smoked paprika and cook for another minute over low heat. Season with salt (or Iberian salt) and pepper. Remove the mushrooms from the pan and set aside. Sauté the remaining beans for 1–2 minutes in the same oil and add to the vegetable stew. If there is any oil left in the skillet, add this as well and if needed, add more salt and pepper. Serve the bean stew in a deep plate and top off with some of the sautéed mushrooms.

A typical red wine from northern Spain such as a Mencia wine from El Bierzo.

¡Gazpacho cremoso y sedoso!
— Creamy, silky gazpacho —

Gazpacho is one of the most iconic and healthy dishes in Spanish cuisine. The farmers from the scorching hot plains of Andalucía have been eating this nutritious cold soup since the 15th century.

The wife of Napoleon II, Eugenia de Montijo, came from Andalucía (Granada) and it is thanks to her that gazpacho became popular in France around 1850. This was the first step towards a worldwide trend.

There are many varieties of this delicious and refreshing summer soup. In Spain the gazpacho often has a more full-bodied and creamier flavor than it does abroad. Probably because the Spanish don't skimp on the olive oil. My family members in Ibiza actually add some mayonnaise to their gazpacho. They will even throw in a handful of pine nuts to make it that much creamier. Definitely worth trying.

Serves 6-8

1 slice of white bread without crust (preferably a day old)
2 lb/1 kg ripe tomatoes
1 (red) onion
1 piece of cucumber (2.5 oz)
1 red bell pepper
½ -1 clove garlic
½ cup/100 ml of water
salt
6 tbsp of extra virgin olive oil
2 tbsp (Sherry) vinegar
1 tbsp mayonnaise
black pepper

Optional:
1 tbsp pine nuts

Soak the bread in a little bit of water and then squeeze out the excess moisture. Cut the tomatoes and onions into large chunks. Peel the cucumber and cut into large chunks. Halve the bell pepper and deseed it. Remove the germ of the garlic clove. Use a blender to puree all these ingredients with the water and a pinch of salt until it becomes a smooth mixture. Add pine nuts for a creamier flavor. Pass through a sieve to achieve an even smoother texture. Mix in the olive oil, vinegar and mayonnaise with a spatula. Season with salt and pepper. Chill for at least one hour in the refrigerator and serve cold.

Serving suggestions:
- Garnish with finely chopped raw veggies, croutons or crispy bits of baked Serrano ham
- Drizzle with (smoked) olive oil

Variations:
- Substitute the fresh garlic with roasted garlic (see recipe on page 166).
- Substitute the onions with 1 spring onion.
- Broil the chunks of tomatoes, onion, bell pepper and the garlic with a pinch of salt and olive oil for 40 minutes at 350°F/180°C.
- Replace ¼ of the tomatoes with strawberries or watermelon. If the gazpacho becomes too watery add an additional slice of bread.
- Add a few drops of honey or a dash of cumin to the gazpacho.

A light red wine (Tempranillo, Joven), a dry Rosado (Spanish rosé), or your favorite Sherry.

¡Sopa de lentejas vegetariana!
— Vegetarian lentil soup —

As soon as the outside temperature drops, nothing beats a warm plate of lentil soup. In Spain they call it a *plato de cuchara*, a dish you eat with a spoon. It is not only delicious but has the added benefit of being very healthy. And, if you'd like to spice it up a little, add one of the suggested garnishes.

Serves 4–8
1 onion
1¼ cup/150 g carrots
1 red bell pepper
½ fennel bulb
2 tomatoes
½ garlic bulb
8 tbsp olive oil
1 tsp cumin seeds
2 tsp smoked paprika (use only 1 tsp when adding chorizo crumble)
2 bay leaves
2 tsp balsamic or Sherry vinegar
2 cups/400 g dark green Spanish lentils
4–6 cups /1–1½ l water (depending on how thick you would like the soup to be)
salt
pepper

Garnishes:

-Chorizo crumble-
2 oz/50 g piece of Spanish chorizo (dried and cured sausage)
2 tbsp olive oil
2 slices/50 g bread
¼ tsp cumin seeds
1 tbsp balsamic vinegar

-Fried plantain-
1 tsp smoked paprika
½ tsp dried thyme
½ tsp dried oregano
¼ tsp garlic powder
¼ tsp salt
1 plantain
2 tbsp olive oil

-Chorizo-shrimp skewers-
juice of one lime
4 tbsp olive oil
1 tbsp honey
1 tsp smoked paprika
Salt
5 oz/150 g Spanish chorizo (dried and cured sausage)
24 large shrimp, unpeeled
8 wooden skewers

Chop all the vegetables finely. Cut a garlic bulb in half horizontally and place one half in a soup pot with 8 tbsp of cold olive oil and a pinch of salt. Slowly heat the oil and sauté the garlic for 2 minutes until it is golden brown. The garlic will flavor the oil. Add the chopped onion, carrot, pepper and fennel. Sauté for about 10 minutes over medium-high heat. Add the cumin seeds, the smoked paprika, the chopped tomatoes and the bay leaves. The juices of the tomatoes will keep the smoked paprika from burning. Sauté for 1 minute over medium-high heat. Deglaze with the balsamic vinegar. Turn up the heat for about 20 seconds. Remove the garlic, add the lentils and stir well. Pour in the cold water and bring to a boil. Cook for 45 minutes over low to medium-high heat. The lentils should still be al dente. Season with salt and pepper.

Chop the chorizo into small pieces and crumble the bread. Heat the olive oil in a heavy skillet and sauté the chorizo for about 1–2 min over medium-high heat and set aside. Sauté the bread crumbs with the cumin seeds in the same oil for about 1–2 minutes over medium-high heat. Deglaze with the balsamic vinegar and sauté for a few more minutes until the bread is crispy.

Mix the smoked paprika, thyme, oregano, garlic powder and salt in a bowl. Slice the plantain and roll the slices in the herb mixture. Heat the olive oil in a skillet and sauté the plantain slices for about 2–3 minutes per side over medium-high heat until golden brown and crispy. Drain on paper towels.

In a large bowl, mix the lime juice, olive oil, honey, smoked paprika and a pinch of salt. Slice the chorizo into 24 thin slices and remove the skin. Alternately skewer 3 shrimp and 3 chorizo slices onto the wooden sticks. You should end up with 8 skewers in total. Brush the skewers with the dressing and sauté for 2 minutes in a (grill) pan over high heat.

A full-bodied red Tempranillo such as a Ribera del Duero Crianza.

¡Sopa de ajo!
— Garlic soup —

This simple soup from La Mancha, home of Don Quixote, comes in several varieties. The basic ingredients are always bread, garlic and olive oil. Nowadays garlic is considered a super food but in the old days it was peasant food. "Do not eat garlic or onions; for their smell will reveal that you are a peasant," is what Don Quixote said to his squire Sancho Panza. Would Don Quixote have eaten this soup after a hard day of tilting at windmills? In any case, I have eaten this soup many times after a hard day or night with too much wine. In the Barrio Húmedo, the place to party if you are in the town of León, sopa de ajo is served in clay bowls to give the party animals a chance to recover from a night out drinking. It is not a refined soup, but it is very tasty. My version with the egg yolk is a bit more elegant.

Serves 4

3.5 oz/100 g Spanish chorizo (dried and cured sausage)
½ lb/200 g day-old bread
6 tbsp olive oil
4 crushed garlic cloves
1 tsp rosemary
2 bay leaves
2 tsp smoked paprika
4 cups/1 l water
salt
2 ripe tomatoes

Cut the chorizo and the bread into small pieces. Heat the olive oil in a soup pot over low heat and sauté the crushed garlic for a few minutes. Add the chorizo and sauté for another 2 minutes over medium-high heat until crunchy. Add the rosemary, the bay leaves and the smoked paprika and sauté for another minute making sure the smoked paprika doesn't burn. Remove the mixture from the pan and set aside. Sauté the pieces of bread in the remaining oil until crunchy and golden. The bread will absorb almost all the oil. Add the chorizo mixture to the pan and stir well. Remove a third of the mixture from the pan (except the garlic) and set aside. Add the water and the tomatoes with a pinch of salt. Let it cook for about 15 minutes over low heat. Remove the bay leaves and puree the soup until silky smooth. Sprinkle the remaining chorizo and bread mixture on top.

Serving suggestion: Place an egg yolk in a soup plate or bowl. Pour the hot soup around the yolk and garnish with the remaining chorizo and bread mixture.

Vegetarian variation: Instead of chorizo, add 1 extra teaspoon of smoked paprika when sautéing the garlic.

A full-bodied Tempranillo, such as a Rioja Crianza or a good wine from La Mancha.

¡Tortilla de patatas!
— Spanish omelet —

At one point in my life I was completely turned off by a certain guy because of his *tortilla de patatas*. The man in question, let's call him Harry, was rich and good looking but his tortilla was a disaster. The way to my heart is most definitely through my stomach and this man got completely lost. For one, he pre-cooked the potatoes to save time. Shocking! Why? Cooking potatoes also takes time. To add insult to injury, he added bananas to the tortilla. The romance ended there.

My husband knows this story. He knows how I loathe a bad tortilla de patatas.
He doesn't even try to prepare this dish and leaves it up to me.
When we are in Spain, we hunt for a good tortilla de patatas. We know knew exactly where you can find really good ones anywhere between Santiago de Compostela and Ibiza. I love it when the tortilla is still a little soft or even runny on the inside.

The tortilla *española*, also known as the tortilla de patatas, is a thick omelet made with potatoes, eggs and olive oil. There are several theories about its origins. Some say it was invented in the Americas during the Spanish occupation in the 16th century. After all, the potato was brought to Europe from the New World by the Spanish explorers. Supposedly, the idea of adding potatoes to whisked eggs was invented to fill the empty bellies of the soldiers.
The tortilla de patatas is first described in a letter addressed to the court of Navarra in 1817. The letter documents the poor living circumstances of the peasants in the highlands. After listing the scarce food resources of the peasants, the tortilla is mentioned as a small pie or a thick omelet made of some eggs, potatoes and breadcrumbs. Peasant food.

Nowadays there are many different varieties of the tortilla de patatas. From the traditional tortilla without onion to the (stuffed) varieties with vegetables, chorizo, fish and even oysters or truffle. I have even tasted tortilla with croissant and Iberian ham in Barcelona. Oh my god, this was absolutely delicious. If Harry had prepared this tortilla, I might have married him.

My Spanish family can have hour-long debates about whether or not onions belong in a tortilla. They will drive 40 miles from Santiago de Compostela to the village of Betanzos just to have a tortilla de patatas for lunch. The Betanzos tortilla has only 4 ingredients: eggs, potatoes (Kennebec), extra virgin olive oil and salt. It is runny on the inside and is made without onions.

I like to prepare my tortilla with onion and sometimes add a pinch of smoked paprika. When my Spanish family got wind of this, I instantly understood how Jamie Oliver must have felt when all of Spain attacked him for adding chorizo to paella.
He broke with tradition, just like I am doing. I think traditions can be broken every now and then, as long as it tastes good.

Serves 4

1 lb / 500 g potatoes
(preferably Kennebec)
1 onion
1¼ cup / 300 ml olive oil
salt
5 large eggs

Optional:
smoked paprika

Peel and rinse the potatoes. Cut them into irregular slices about ¼-inch thick and 1 to 1-½ inches long. Finely chop the onion. Heat the olive oil in a heavy skillet. Test the temperature of the oil by tossing in a bit of bread. When it instantly turns golden brown, the oil is at the right temperature. Fry the potatoes and the onion for about 13 minutes over low to medium-high heat. (Make sure you use plenty of olive oil, the potatoes should be covered). Turn up the heat for the last 2 minutes and fry the potatoes until the edges are browned. The onion should not brown. Drain the potatoes in a colander, saving the oil. Salt the potatoes and set aside to cool off. Whisk the eggs but do not salt them. Salt alters the structure of the eggs, changes the color and makes then more liquid. Combine the potatoes and onions with the eggs, and let it sit for a few minutes. For some extra kick, add a pinch of smoked paprika. Heat 2 tbsp of the olive oil you used before in the same skillet, add the potato egg mixture and fry the tortilla for 30 seconds over high heat. (Using a spatula. press down the edges of the tortilla to get a nice rounded shape). Sprinkle with a bit of salt. Place a large plate on the skillet and flip the pan so the tortilla winds up on the plate. Slide the tortilla back in the skillet with the cooked side up. Cook for another 30 seconds over medium-high heat. Place the plate back on the skillet, flip the tortilla again and cook for another 10 seconds over medium-high heat.

Note: Instructions above are for a tortilla that is still runny on the inside. If you like a firmer tortilla, cook it longer on each side.
-30 seconds each side = runny
-1 to 5 minutes each side = firm

Serving suggestion:
-If you want to serve the tortilla in pieces as a tapa, prepare the firmer version
-Delicious with salsa romesco (see recipe on page 176) or roasted pepper sauce (see recipe on page 124)

A tortilla de patatas can be served hot or cold at any kind of occasion, fancy or casual. Bring a tortilla to a picnic, serve it as an appetizer, a main course, a tapa or a pincho.

When preparing tapas or pinchos, you can mix and match with a slice of bread, a slice of tortilla, a dollop of aioli (see recipes on page 166), a Padron pepper (see recipe on page 70), a roasted bell pepper, or a black olive.

Variation: tear up a croissant and add this to the whisked eggs with a few strips of Serrano or Iberian ham.

🍷 A young red Tempranillo or a Spanish beer.

¡Huevos estrellados!
— Scrumptious fried eggs —

'Shattered' eggs is the literal translation of this classic dish which is served in many restaurants in Madrid. Whenever I see it listed on the menu, I always order it and every time I am 'shattered' by the flavor of the egg yolks mixed with the fries. It's very easy to prepare and not expensive.

Serves 2–3

-Spanish fries-
3 medium-sized new potatoes
2 cups/500 ml olive oil

-Eggs-
2-3 eggs
salt
1 egg yolk

Peel the potatoes, cut into fries and place them in a bowl filled with water. Drain the water and dry the fries. Heat the olive oil in a heavy skillet. Once the oil is hot, add the fries, lower the heat and fry for about 15 minutes over low to medium heat until cooked. Every now and then stir carefully. Turn up to heat and fry for another few minutes until golden and crunchy. Remove the fries from the pan and let them drain on a paper towel.

Fry the eggs in the same pan for about 1–2 minutes over high heat until the egg white is set but the yolk is still runny.
Place the French fries on a plate and sprinkle with salt. Pour the raw egg yolk over the fries and toss. Place the fried eggs on top of the fries and break the yolks. Finish off with a pinch of salt.

Serving suggestion: Add some crispy Serrano ham (see recipe page 118) and/or grated truffle.

🍷 A Catalan wine such as a Costers del Segre or a Terra Alta. If you have added the truffle, serve a more full-bodied wine such as a Toro.

¡Patatas bravas!
— Fried potato cubes with a spicy sauce —

Patatas bravas, sautéed potatoes with a spicy sauce is a classic Spanish dish and a popular tapa or ración (larger portion than a tapa). The word *brava* refers to the spicy sauce. Salsa brava comes in two variations, with or without tomatoes. I like to make it without tomatoes, the way it is made in Ponferrada, my family's home town in the North of Spain. The main ingredient of this salsa brava is the pimentón, or smoked paprika (both the sweet variety and the spicy kind) which gives the sauce a nice, warm, red color and a smoky flavor with a pleasant kick. This is the most authentic kind of salsa brava but it's a bit of an acquired taste since the smoked paprika flavor is strong. Feel free to use more or less of the spicy or the sweet smoked paprika depending on your taste buds. In Catalonia they serve aioli with patatas bravas. My favorite aioli contains Sichuan pepper. My Spanish and Chinese worlds come together in this dish.

Serves 2–4

-Salsa brava-
2 cups/½ l water
1 bouillon cube (chicken or vegetable)
2/3 cup/100 g onion
1–2 tbsp smoked paprika (sweet)
1–2 tbsp smoked paprika (spicy)
regular paprika powder
1/3 cup/40 g all-purpose flour
salt

-Patatas bravas-
2 large potatoes
olive oil
salt

Heat the water in a saucepan and add the bouillon cube. Finely chop the onion. Heat the olive oil in a skillet and sauté the onion for 5–8 minutes over low to medium-high heat. Add both kinds of smoked paprika. Stir well and don't let it burn. Add the flour, mix well and sauté for about 2 minutes. Pour in the bouillon bit by bit, keep stirring to prevent lumps. Bring the sauce to a boil, cover and let it cook for about 10 minutes. Season with salt and puree until smooth.

Peel the potatoes, rinse and dry. Cut them in irregular cubes about 1 inch each. Heat the olive oil in a heavy skillet. When the oil starts to smoke, carefully place the potato cubes in the pan. Sauté for about. 8–10 minutes until they are soft on the inside. Turn up the heat and fry the potatoes for about 2 minutes until they are golden brown and crispy on the outside. They should be soft on the inside and crunchy on the outside. Drain on a paper towel. Sprinkle with salt. Serve with the warm salsa brava and the aioli with Sichuan pepper (optional, see recipe on page 166).

🍷 A light red wine (a Tempranillo such as a Rioja Joven) or a Spanish beer.

¡Pimientos de Padrón!
— Fried Padron peppers —

The little green pepper called 'pimiento de Padrón', also known as 'pimiento de Herbón', gets its name from the town of Padrón in Galicia in the northwest of Spain. This variety of the Capsicum annuum was already being cultivated in 16th century by missionaries in the town of Herbón right next to Padrón. The missionaries had brought the pepper plants back from the New World. It would seem that the missionaries liked a bit of spice or rather culinary roulette. One in every ten pimientos is *very* spicy. The hot flavor of a pepper is caused by capsaicin, a chemical compound the pepper produces as protection against insects and other animals. Not all peppers produce this compound. So why are only some peppers hot? This is caused by several factors, including climate and the amount of water and irrigation methods. Within one harvest, it could be that some peppers got more water or sunlight than others. Some experts claim that the pointier, less shiny peppers are the hottest.

When I was a young girl, children were not allowed to eat the pimientos de Padrón the grown-ups had ordered. What if we burned our mouths! Instead we would be served *cacahuetes* (peanuts in the shell) and *gaseosa* (Spanish soda) with a dash of red wine. My family would not prepare the peppers at home since you could buy them on any street corner. We would always hope that one of the adults would get a hot one. Unfortunately, I never saw this happen.

Serves 4

1 lb/500 g pimientos de Padrón
10 tbsp extra virgin olive oil
coarse sea salt

Heat the olive oil in a heavy frying pan. Add the pimientos one by one. Never all at the same time because then they will not cook properly. The pimientos should float in the oil. Cover the pan since the peppers contain water and this will make them spatter. Fry the pimientos for about 2 minutes on either side over medium-high heat until golden brown. Keep turning. When they start to blister, they are done. Let the pimientos drain on paper towel. Sprinkle with sea salt and serve warm.

A light red Tempranillo such as a Rioja Joven. Or a Spanish beer.

¡Ensaladilla rusa vegetal!
— Vegetarian Russian potato salad —

According to lore, this Russian potato salad was invented in a posh Russian restaurant in the 19th century. In addition to potatoes, other ingredients used were: veal tongue, smoked duck, crayfish and caviar. The white mayonnaise supposedly was a nod to the snow-capped Russian mountains. This dish is a very popular tapa throughout Spain and can be found in any tapas bar or restaurant. In my experience, even an average roadside restaurant serves a good *ensaladilla rusa*. I like to prepare my version with purple potatoes for their wonderful color and the black sesame seeds are a nod to the caviar in the original 19th century recipe.

Serves 4

-Ensaladilla-
1 lb/450 g (purple) potatoes
5 oz/130 g carrots
4 oz/110 g frozen peas
2 roasted peppers from a jar
¼ cup/25 g pitted black olives
salt and pepper
2 eggs
2 spring onions
1 tbsp black sesame seeds

Optional
3 oz/75 g canned tuna (in oil)

-Lime mayonnaise-
1 egg
1 tsp Dijon mustard
salt
black pepper
few drops of lime juice
¾ cup/150 ml sunflower oil

Boil the unpeeled potatoes with a pinch of salt for about 20 minutes. Don't overcook them, they should still be al dente. Do the same with the carrots in a separate pan. Blanch the peas for 1 minute and run under cold water. Peel the potatoes and then cut them, along with the carrots, into ½ inch cubes. Slice the grilled peppers into ½-inch pieces. Finely chop the olives. Carefully combine the potatoes, carrots, peppers and olives and season with salt and pepper. Boil the eggs in cold water with salt (to avoid cracking) for 9 minutes over low to medium-high heat and cool in ice water. Peel the eggs and remove the yolks in their entirety and set aside. Cut the cooked egg whites in pieces and carefully mix into the potato salad. If you like your potato salad with tuna, you can add some chunks at this point.

Place the egg, mustard, salt, pepper and a few drops of lime juice in the container of a hand-held mixer. Mix and slowly pour in the sunflower oil until the mayonnaise is emulsified.

Stir five tablespoons of the lime mayonnaise into the potato salad. Grate the cooked egg yolks on top and garnish with some slices spring onion and the black sesame seeds.

Variation: Add 1 tbsp of the liquid from the roasted pepper jar to the mayonnaise.

Serving suggestion:
Serve on a piece of bread as a tapa and garnish with some boiled quail eggs.

A young red wine, such as a Rioja Joven.

¡Coca de escalivada!
— Ibiza-style pizza with grilled vegetables —

The word *coca* supposedly derives from the Dutch word *koek*, the English word *cake* and the German word *Kuchen* and dates from the era when Catalonia was part of Charles V's Holy Roman Empire. This rectangular pizza used to be made from the remnants of bread dough.

You have to add a liberal quantity of olive oil to the dough. The exciting thing about this recipe is that you can prepare the dough without measuring the amount of flour just by feeling the consistency while kneading (although for this recipe I did measure the flour). I used to watch a Catalonian baker do this. He just kept on kneading until the dough suddenly became a ball, leaving his hands completely clean. He explained: "You just have to knead the dough until it sticks." At the time I didn't understand what he meant. Now I do.

When we were teenagers, my girlfriends and I used to visit this bakery often. The real reason was the baker's good-looking son. Nothing ever happened between any of us and the baker's son, but I still prepare coca dough the same way his father did.

You can buy this delicious snack in almost every bakery in Catalonia and the Balearic Islands. Every region has its own version. For the holidays, bakeries bake special sweet cocas.

The *coca de escalivada* is one of the most traditional cocas and is made following an age-old Catalonian recipe. The name comes from the cooking method: *escalivar* means to cook over hot ashes. These days we just roast the vegetables in the oven.

When I'm in Ibiza I always prepare this coca with the delicious bell peppers from our vegetable garden. I always start with the escalivada and while the vegetables are roasting, I prepare the dough.

Serves 6–8

-Escalivada-
3 red bell peppers
1 eggplant
1 red onion, peeled
olive oil
coarse sea salt
black pepper

-Dough-
2 cups/200 g all-purpose flour
1 cup/200 ml lukewarm water
½ cup/100 ml olive oil
1 tbsp salt
extra olive oil and flour
coarse sea salt

optional:
½ packet (3.5 g) dry yeast
cardamom

Preheat the oven to 425°F/220°C. Pierce the peppers and the eggplants a few times with a fork to prevent them from bursting in the oven. Brush the peppers, eggplant and onion with olive oil. Place them on a baking tray and roast for about 30 minutes until the vegetables are cooked. Remove from the oven and allow to cool. Remove the skin and the seeds from the pepper and the eggplant. Cut all the vegetables into thin strips and place them in a bowl.

Preheat the oven to 480°F/250°C. Pour the flour, water, olive oil (and the yeast), in a bowl and knead the dough until it sticks together and not to your hands. The dough should be smooth, elastic and oily. Add a bit more flour if it still sticks to your hands.

Let the dough rest for about 15 minutes. Flatten the dough with your hands into a ½-inch thick rectangle and place it on a baking sheet lined with parchment paper. This is actually quite easy. Spread the roasted vegetables on top of the dough. I like to make a diagonal pattern. Sprinkle with coarse sea salt and drizzle with olive oil. Place the tray in the oven for about 20 minutes until the dough is done and crispy. Cut into rectangular pieces. If you like, add a pinch of cardamom for a citrus like touch.

Serving suggestion: Makes for a great snack, with a salad or a soup

🍷 A typical Catalonian red wine such as a Somontano, Costers del Segre or a Terra Alta. Or a red wine from Ibiza!

¡Migas con uvas y secreto ibérico!
— Chorizo croutons with grapes and Iberian pork secreto —

Spanish cuisine has been influenced by several cultures, but the Moors had the biggest culinary impact. From 711 AD onwards, the Moors occupied most of Spain. Over the course of the following centuries the Moors were driven out of Spain by the Christian Kings. The fall of Granada in 1492 marked the end of the Moorish Era.

Migas de Pastor literally means 'shepherd's crumbs' because sheep herders used to make this dish from their leftover bread. Some say couscous was the inspiration for this dish, but that Spanish Christians made it with bread and pork to distinguish it from Moorish food. In ancient times, the Spanish Kings supposedly loved this peasant dish. There are many regional variations of migas. I love the combination with grapes.

Serves 4

-Chorizo croutons with grapes-
2 slices day-old bread
2 oz/50 g chorizo (Spanish dried and cured sausage)
1 garlic clove
1 tbsp olive oil
salt
black pepper
½ tsp (dried) thyme
¼ tsp smoked paprika
2 oz/50 g grapes (red and/or white)

-Caramelized Iberian pork secreto-
14 oz/400 g Iberian pork secreto
coarse sea salt
sugar
thyme
smoked paprika
Iberian salt (see recipe on page 174)
4 quail eggs

Crumble the bread or cut it into tiny pieces and wet with some water. If you have the time, cover the moist bread and let it sit for a few hours. Cut the chorizo into small pieces. Chop the garlic. Heat the olive oil in a heavy skillet and sauté the garlic for 1 to 2 minutes over low heat. Add the chorizo first, followed by the bread and sauté over medium-high heat until the mixture is crunchy (8–15 minutes) Add a pinch of salt and pepper, the thyme and the smoked paprika. Halve the grapes and place them on top of the migas.

Secreto Ibérico means Iberian pork secreto and it refers to the juiciest cut of the Iberian pig. This is one of the centerpieces of Spanish cuisine, possibly because the diet of this pig consists of acorns, berries and herbs. It is a highly marbled cut from the area between the shoulder blade and the loin. It has a beautiful pink color and a silky texture.

Cut the secreto into 1-inch slices. Sprinkle with coarse salt. Heat up a heavy grill pan with ridges and cook the slices over high heat without oil for 3–4 minutes on each side. Make sure the secreto stays pink on the inside. Remove the meat from the pan and sprinkle with a bit of sugar. Using a crème brûlée torch, burn the sugar until it is caramelized. Cut the secreto into smaller pieces, season with a pinch of thyme, smoked paprika and Iberian salt. Serve the chorizo croutons with the *secreto ibérico* and the fried quail eggs.

Vegetarian variation:
Leave out the chorizo and the *secreto ibérico* and use extra smoked paprika (about ½–1 tsp).

Variations:
- serve the *secreto ibérico* with saffron mashed potatoes (see recipe on page 158) and/or salsa romesco (see recipe on page 176)
- serve as a tapa: take a slice of bread or pan con tomate (see recipe on page 38), spread it with pepper or tomato jelly (see recipe on page 172 and 45) and place a slice of *secreto ibérico* on top.

🍷 A full-bodied red wine such as a Ribera del Duero.

¡Pan payés fácil ibicenco!
— Easy peasant bread from Ibiza —

My favorite bakery on Ibiza bakes a peasant-style bread that is firm and low in salt. I love this bread, especially with aioli (see recipe on page 166) and marinated olives (see recipe on page 44), the way it is served in many bars and restaurants on Ibiza. Any normal person would carry some souvenirs or a chorizo home from a vacation in Spain but I always pack a loaf of this bread in my suitcase. Back home, I slice it and freeze it so I can enjoy it as long as possible. On special occasions, I defrost it and prepare aioli so I can feel like I am in Ibiza. I guess you could call this my guilty pleasure.

4 cups/500 g all-purpose flour plus a little extra for sprinkling
1 to 1½ tsp salt
1 packet of dry yeast (7 g)
1¼ cup/300 ml water

Combine the flour with the salt and the yeast in a big bowl. Add the water and mix well with a wooden spoon in preparation for kneading. As soon as the spoon starts to stick, the dough is ready for kneading. Sprinkle some flour on a flat surface. Knead the dough for about 5 to 10 minutes until it is smooth and elastic. It can be a little sticky. Shape the dough into a ball and drop it on your work surface. If the ball keeps its shape, the dough is ready. Cover the bowl with a damp cloth and let it rest for about 1 hour in a warm, dry place until doubled in size. Preheat the oven to 385 °F /195 °C. Flatten the dough a couple of times, knead it for a few minutes and mold it into a round shape. Sprinkle the top and the bottom with some flour. Using a knife, cut a few incisions in the top of the bread. Let it rest for another 10 minutes, place the bread on a baking sheet and bake for about 30 minutes until golden and crunchy.

Variation: Substitute half of the all-purpose flour with whole wheat, spelt, kamut or rye flour.

In Spain the most commonly used flour is *harina de fuerza* which is made from hard wheat. This contains more gluten, which allows the dough to rise fully and gives the bread the right structure. I use an all-purpose flour, which is a blend of hard and soft wheat but I also like to combine it with other types of flour.

¡Paella valenciana !
— Paella from Valencia —

A traditional paella Valenciana only has ten ingredients: chicken, rabbit, flat beans, garrofón (Spanish-style butter beans), tomato, rice, olive oil, water, saffron and salt. There are several local versions featuring escargots, artichoke, rosemary or garlic. All these ingredients are native to each particular region.

Another interesting detail is that you should always eat paella with a wooden spoon. Investing in a paella pan is definitely worthwhile, but you can also prepare paella in a large frying pan.

I prefer to make a version without rabbit, which in all other aspects is very similar to the traditional paella Valenciana. When using butter beans and escargots, I go for the canned and frozen ones just to make things easier. You can prepare a delicious paella with a few simple ingredients without having to hunt for fresh escargots.

Serves 3-4
1 tsp saffron threads
(about 10-20 threads)
¾ cups/150g flat beans
1 ripe tomato
2 cloves garlic
½ lb/250 g chicken thighs
3 tbsp olive oil
salt
¼ cup/50 g canned butter beans
1 tsp pimentón (smoked paprika)
1 packet of paella seasoning (0,14 oz)
2 cups/500 ml hot water
1 cup/200 g paella rice
3 sprigs of rosemary
1 lemon

Optional:
8 frozen escargots with herb butter

Mix the saffron threads with 2 tablespoons of water and heat this for 20 seconds in the microwave. This will enhance the flavor and color. Cut or break the flat beans into big chunks about 1.5 inches long. Grate the tomato. Crush and mince the garlic cloves. Dice the chicken into 1-inch cubes and season with salt. Heat the olive oil in a (paella) pan with a pinch of salt to prevent spattering. Sauté the chicken for about 5 minutes over medium-high heat until it is browned and crispy.

Add the flat beans, the butter beans, the minced garlic, the tomato, the smoked paprika and the paella seasoning. Reduce the heat and stir well. Add the 2 cups of warm water and let it simmer for 20 minutes over low heat. The flavors need to have time to blend together to enhance the taste of the stock. Taste and season with salt. Add the saffron. Gently spoon the rice into the stock. Turn up the heat and bring to a boil and let it cook for 2 minutes. Reduce the heat and let it simmer for 20-25 minutes until the rice is cooked. If necessary, add some more water (about ½ cup). Place the rosemary sprigs on top. Do not stir! It is important that when all the liquid has been absorbed the rice is still al dente. The kernels should feel dry and loose. When using escargots, preheat the oven (while the paella is cooking) and prepare them according to the directions on the packaging. In order to get a crispy crust on the bottom of the pan (known as *socarrat*), pour 1 tbsp of olive oil over the rice. The oil will sink to the bottom of the pan allowing the rice to get a little 'fried'. Remove the pan from the heat and cover the paella with a newspaper. Let it rest for a few minutes. Serve with lemon wedges.

Preparation suggestion: The rice to water ratio is 1:3 but start with 2 cups of water. Have some more hot water on hand so that you can add (1/2 cup) as needed if the all the stock has been absorbed but the rice is not yet done.

A full bodied white wine such as a Penedès Chardonnay or a Rueda Superior/Centenario. For red wine lovers: a light Tempranillo such as a Rioja *Joven* (young) or *Crianza* (aged).

¡Chorizos ibéricos a la sidra con col verde!
— Cabbage rolls with Iberian sausage —

Every now and then you should have a cheat day and enjoy food that is just plain bad for you. This recipe was inspired by a classic dish from Asturias: *chorizo a la sidra*. Fresh Iberian sausage, slow-cooked in hard cider. The cider gives the sausage a special flavor and the sauce is wonderful for dipping. For my version, I add a little bit of green by wrapping the sausage in Savoy cabbage. It adds a touch of color and makes me feel less guilty.

Serves 4

Salt
4 Savoy cabbage leaves
4 fresh Iberian sausages
3 tbsp/50 ml hard cider
1 tbsp honey
5 black peppercorns

Preheat the oven to 350°F/180°C. Bring a pan of water to a boil. Add a pinch of salt and blanch the cabbage leaves for 5 minutes over high heat until they are cooked but are still al dente. Remove the cabbage leaves from the pan and allow to cool. Place the sausages, the cider, the honey and the peppercorns in a baking dish. Score the sausages to allow most of the fat to escape. Place the dish in the oven for about 20 minutes. Then, roll each sausage in a cabbage leaf. Cut the rolls into 2-inch pieces and pin each piece with a skewer.

Variation: Heat 1 tbsp olive oil in a skillet and sauté the rolls for about 2 minutes until golden brown on all sides.

A red Tempranillo, such as a Ribero del Duero Crianza.

¡Albóndigas con salsa sedosa!
— Spanish meatballs with a silky tomato-saffron sauce —

Many Spanish dishes have Arabic roots. This is no surprise since the Moors from Northern Africa occupied most of Spain from 711 to 1492 AD. Traces of Moorish influence can still be found in Spanish architecture, language and cuisine. This dish most definitely has Arabic roots. *Albúnduga* means hazelnut in Arabic (*avellana* in Spanish) which refers to the round shape of the meatballs.

As with all classics, every family, mother, grandmother, aunt, neighbor, tapas bar, ex and (ex)mother-in-law has his or her own version of these meatballs and sauce. Everyone claims their version is the best or the most authentic. No two meatballs taste the same. They are great as a tapa, a pincho or a ración (larger portion). I like to jazz my meatballs up a little by adding saffron to the sauce. The saffron adds flavor, color, depth and a touch of class. I would strongly suggest first preparing the *picada* (a quintessentially Spanish mixture used to thicken soups and sauces), followed by the sauce, saving the meatballs for last.

Makes 25

-Picada-
1 garlic clove
¼ tsp coarse sea salt
1 tbsp pine nuts or hazelnuts
1 handful flat-leaf parsley

-Tomato-saffron sauce-
6–8 saffron threads
2/3 cup/150 ml warm water
2 tomatoes
1 onion
2 tbsp olive oil
¼ tsp salt
1 tbsp bread crumbs or ¾ tbsp all-purpose flour
¼ cup/50 ml white wine

- Albóndigas-
2 slices/50 g (whole grain) bread
1 fl oz/30 ml Pedro Ximénez, sweet Sherry, Port or red wine
1 tsp salt
1 tsp black pepper
1 handful flat-leaf parsley, chopped
1 garlic clove, crushed or ½ tsp garlic powder
1 egg
½ lb/250 g ground pork
½ lb/250 g ground beef
All-purpose flour or bread crumbs
2 tbsp olive oil

Using a mortar and pestle, grind the garlic and salt into a paste. Add the pine nuts/hazelnuts and parsley and puree everything in a blender into a smooth paste.

Soak the saffron in the warm water. Grate the tomatoes and finely chop the onions, Heat the olive oil in a skillet and sauté the onion for about 8 minutes over medium-high heat until caramelized. Add the tomatoes and sauté for another 2 minutes over medium-high heat. Add the breadcrumbs or the flour and mix well. Deglaze with the white wine and let it simmer for 1 minute. Pour in the water with saffron and let the sauce simmer for about 15 more minutes. Puree the sauce until smooth.

Soak the bread for 5 minutes in the Pedro Ximénez until it is saturated and soft. Mix the meat, salt, pepper, parsley, garlic, egg and bread together in a bowl. Form into 1-inch meatballs. Roll them in the flour or the bread crumbs. Heat the olive oil in a heavy skillet. Sauté the meatballs for 5 minutes on each side over medium-high heat until golden brown.

Add the albóndigas and the picada to the sauce and cook for about 5 minutes over low heat.

Variations:
-Use pure ground beef instead of a mixture of pork and beef
-Substitute the saffron with turmeric.
-Substitute the whole grain bread with white bread
-Substitute the alcohol with milk

🍷 A full-bodied red wine such as a Ribera del Duero Crianza.

¡Cordero asado estilo Segovia!
— Roast leg of lamb Segovian style —

Roast lamb reminds me of my honeymoon, a road trip across Spain. We started in the Basque country and, since we loved the food there so much, my husband and I were convinced that romance and good food were a match made in heaven.
Halfway through our trip we wound up in Segovia where many restaurants serve a leg of lamb roasted in special (oak) wood-fired ovens. We were seduced by the delicious aroma coming from one little restaurant. It was late and were starving. Their lamb was prepared with lard, salt, garlic and water. The meat was so moist and tender it just melted in our mouths. Pure love.

Serves 6–8

1 leg of lamb about 3 lbs/1½ kg
salt
black pepper
4 tbsp/50 g lard, butter or olive oil
6–8 garlic cloves
1 tsp (dried) rosemary, plus extra
1 tsp (dried) thyme, plus extra
½ cup/100 ml water
½ cup/100 ml white wine
5 potatoes
2 onions
2 tbsp flat-leaf parsley
coarse sea salt

Preheat the oven to 330°F/165°C. Sprinkle the lamb with salt and pepper. Rub the lamb all over with the lard, butter or olive oil. Place the lamb in a roasting pan. Flatten the unpeeled garlic with the side of a knife and add to the pan together with the rosemary and thyme. Pour in the wine and water and place the pan in the oven.
After 30 minutes, turn the lamb over and, if needed, add some more water, wine and lard/butter/olive oil. There should always be layer of liquid in the roasting pan. Roast for another 30 minutes. In the meantime, peel and slice the potatoes and the onions and sprinkle with salt and pepper. Remove the roasting pan from the oven and take out the lamb. Raise the temperature to 400°F/200°C. Peel the garlic cloves that remained in the pan and squeeze them into the liquid in the pan. Place the potato and onion slices and the parsley in the pan. Sprinkle with some coarse sea salt. Place the leg of lamb on top and sprinkle with coarse sea salt and some additional rosemary and thyme. Pour some more wine or water in the pan. Place the pan back in the oven for 60 minutes, basting the lamb every now and then and turning it after 30 minutes. After 60 minutes it should be golden brown and crispy.

🍷 A full-bodied red wine such as a Ribera del Duero Reserva.

¡Rabo de buey con salsa de vino y chocolate!
— Braised Oxtail in a red wine-chocolate sauce —

The first time I tried bull's tail was in Sevilla, in August, in 100°F weather. Sevilla was hot in every sense of the word and the Sevillanos seemed to revel in it. All over town people were dancing, partying, eating and drinking. During our stay I only ate gazpachos and salads since I was so overheated. Except for the last night when we decided to eat at the air-conditioned restaurant in our hotel. The specialty was *rabo de toro*, or bull's tail. Traditionally this dish used to be prepared with the tails of the bulls that had died in the bullring. Since I was tired of salads and had finally cooled off, I decided to try the local favorite. I don't think I spoke a word during the whole meal since I couldn't believe such tender meat existed!

I have prepared a more ethical variation on this dish using oxtail rather than bull's tail. I was inspired to add a chocolate sauce by the traditional wild game recipes from the province of Aragón.

Serves 4

- 1 large onion
- 2 carrots
- 1 leek
- ¼ head of fennel
- 4 garlic cloves
- 2 cups/500 ml red wine
- 4 lbs/2 kg oxtail or chuck roast
- salt
- black pepper
- all-purpose flour
- 7 tbsp olive oil
- ¼ tsp powdered fennel
- ¼ tsp rosemary
- 1 tomato
- ¾ cup/200 ml water
- 1 bay leaf
- 1 oz/25 g dark chocolate (70–80% cacao)

A day in advance: Cut the vegetables and crush the garlic. Place the meat, the vegetables and garlic in a large bowl, pour in the wine and let it marinate overnight.
Marinating the meat tenderizes it and adds flavor.

Dry the meat with a paper towel, sprinkle with salt and pepper and lightly dust with a bit of flour. Heat the olive oil in a large heavy pan and sear the meat on each side for about 3 minutes until browned. Remove from the pan and set aside.

Remove the vegetables and garlic from the marinade and let then drain in a colander. Place the vegetables and the garlic in the oil that is left in the skillet, add the powdered fennel and the rosemary and sauté for about 5 minutes. Chop the tomatoes and add to the pan. Sauté for another 5 minutes over low heat. Add the meat, the red wine from the marinade, and the bay leaf. Let it cook over high heat for 2 minutes, allowing the alcohol to evaporate. Season with salt and pepper. Add water until the meat and the vegetables are covered. Cover the pan and let it simmer for about 4 hours until the meat is tender and falls away from the bone. Check every hour to see if there is enough liquid in the pan, adding water if necessary. The meat must be covered in liquid. Take the meat from the pan and remove all the bones. (per lb/500 gr oxtail I usually wind up with ¼ lb/130 g of meat. Puree the vegetables with the remaining liquid and the chocolate. (The chocolate will give the sauce a more intense flavor and color. You should hardly taste the chocolate so start by adding just a little bit). Add the meat to the sauce. The amount of sauce is meant for about a 1 lb of meat. Check with your butcher beforehand to find out how much oxtail you need in order to have 1 lb of cooked meat left at the end.

Serving suggestion:
- Serve with mashed potatoes (see recipes on page 158) and arugula.
- add some blackberry mayonnaise (see recipe on page 45).

Variation (tapa): Toast a slice of brioche or prepare a pan con tomate (see recipe on page 38) and spread it with some tomato or pepper jelly (see recipes on page 45 and 172). Scoop some of the oxtail meat on top.

🍷 A robust wine such as a Toro Reserva or a Priorat Reserva.

¡Flamenquines de pollo!
— Breaded chicken rolls with saffron mayonnaise —

Flamenquines are an Andalusian specialty and they look like rolled up schnitzel Cordon Bleu. I like to prepare them with chicken. They are easy to prepare, not expensive and a feast for the eyes.

The flamenquin with its golden color owes its name to the blonde locks of the Flemish troops (Flamencos) who accompanied Charles the V in Spain. Everybody always loves these and it doesn't surprise me!

Serves 4

-Saffron mayonnaise-
8-10 saffron threads
2/3 cups/150 ml olive oil
1 egg
salt
a few drops of lemon juice

-Flamenquines-
4 chicken breasts
salt
black pepper
smoked paprika
8 thin slices Serrano or Iberian ham
4 thick slices chorizo
4 slices Manchego cheese
4 strips roasted bell pepper (from a jar)
1 handful of flat-leaf parsley
1 egg
1 cup/125 g all-purpose flour
1½ cup/125 g bread crumbs
olive oil

Optional:
Iberian salt (see recipe on page 174)

Grind the saffron threads into a powder. Pour the olive oil into the container of a hand-held blender. Add the egg, a pinch of salt, the lemon juice and the saffron powder. Place the hand blender in the container. Puree the mixture without lifting the hand blender. Once the mixture has homogenized, continue mixing by lifting the blender up and down until the mayonnaise has reached the desired thickness.

Butterfly each chicken breast by placing it on a cutting board, holding it flat with your non-knife hand and slicing it horizontally without separating the two halves completely. Place some baking paper on the inside of each butterflied breast. Pound with a rolling pin or a meat mallet to an even ¼-inch thickness and sprinkle with some salt, pepper, smoked paprika (or Iberian salt). Place on top of each flattened breast: 2 ham slices, 1 chorizo slice, 1 cheese slice and one bell pepper strip. Roll the breast up like burrito and if needed, secure with toothpick or skewer.

Finely chop the parsley. Whisk the egg with the parsley and a pinch of salt in a shallow bowl. Take two more shallow bowls, filling one with flour and another with bread crumbs.
First roll the flamenquines in the flour, then dip them in the egg and finally roll them in the bread crumbs. Heat a good amount of olive oil in a heavy skillet and sauté the flamenquines for about 3 minutes over medium-high heat. Turn regularly so they brown all around. Lower the heat and cook them for another 3 minutes. The flamenquines should be crunchy on the outside and juicy on the inside. Drain on a paper towel. Slice them into 2-inch pieces.

Serve with saffron mayonnaise

Serving suggestions:
-Serve with a salad and or Spanish fries (see recipe on page 66)
-Add some chorizo slices and some fresh bell pepper strips to the pan for the last two minutes.
-Flavor the bread crumbs with a pinch of smoked paprika and/or garlic powder

🍷 A smooth red such as Rioja (Crianza) or a Ribera del Duero.

¡Empanada gallega de atún!
— Tuna empanada from Galicia —

The taste of empanada brings back my childhood memories of summers spent in Galicia. Since the weather there is just as unpredictable as it is in Holland, a day at the beach was a special outing. On the way there we would stop at a *confitería* (a special bakery) where we would pick up the empanadas which my uncle had ordered ahead of time.

I come from a big family and a day at the beach was always quite an event. We would travel in a caravan of cars along windy roads towards the coast. Grandpa, grandma, aunts, uncles, cousins, a priest and a nanny, all squeezed into a handful of cars. Without seatbelts in those days. The empanadas were stacked on top of the rear shelf and obstructed the view. Nobody cared! We were just like the pilgrims who travelled to Santiago de Compostela. They also took empanadas on their pilgrimage for practical reasons; easy to carry and easy to eat.

We were only allowed to eat the empanada after swimming, otherwise we might get a *corte de digestión (indigestion)*. As a child, I didn't know what this meant but it sounded so serious that we never dared break this rule.

The combination of wet, salty hands and the golden pastry with the delicious filling is etched in my memory. As a child, I decided that one day I was going make my own empanadas.

There are many ways to prepare empanadas and every grandmother, aunt, restaurant or confitería in Galicia has their own recipe. I have had many different empanadas and I have developed a recipe that closely resembles the one from my childhood. I prepared this one for the first audition round of MasterChef Holland.
It must have been good because I passed on to the next round.

Preparing an empanada is an art one has to master. However accurately you follow the recipe, you have to get a feel for it, whether the dough has the right consistency and whether or not the filling is too dry or too moist. Practice makes perfect and the more often you prepare an empanada, the easier it will be.

The wonderful thing about this recipe is that you can experiment with the filling in many different ways. But whether you prepare it with meat, fish or vegetables, the preparation of the dough is always very special. It is prepared with the oil in which you have sautéed the filling. This way, the dough absorbs all the tastes of the filling giving it an intense flavor.

Serves 8–10

-Filling-
2 eggs
3 onions
1 red bell pepper
1 green bell pepper
½ cup/100 ml extra virgin olive oil
1 tsp salt
¼ tsp black pepper
2 tsp flat-leaf parsley
2 cans of tuna in oil

-Dough-
6 tbsp/80 g butter
1 lb/450 g flour
1 packet of dry yeast (7 g)
2/3 cup/150 ml 'leftover' oil from sautéing the filling
just under 1 cup/100 ml white wine
just under 1 cup/100 ml whole milk
1 tsp salt
2–3 tsp smoked paprika
1 egg yolk

Boil the eggs for 10 minutes over low heat and set aside. Finely chop the onions, peppers and the parsley. Heat the olive oil in a heavy frying pan and sauté the onions and peppers seasoned with the salt and pepper for 8–10 minutes over low to medium-high heat. Add the smoked paprika and tomatoes and sauté for another 3 minutes until the tomatoes have softened. Add the tuna with the oil and mix it all together. Pass the mixture through a sieve and catch the oil in a bowl. You will need this for the dough. It should be around 2/3 cup. If you don't have enough, add some fresh olive oil when making the dough.

Variation: Add 3,5 oz of Spanish chorizo (dried and cured sausage) to the vegetables.

Vegetarian variation: Substitute the tuna with tofu (200 g) and wakame (25 g) and sauté this with the vegetables.

Melt the butter. Mix the flour with the yeast in a bowl and make a well in the middle. Pour all the remaining ingredients in the well except for the egg yolk. Mix with one hand or a spatula in a spiral motion, working your way from the inside to the outside until everything is incorporated. Cover the bowl and let the dough rise for about 60 minutes in a warm spot. Preheat the oven to 350°F/180°C. Sprinkle some flour on your work surface and knead the dough for about 5 minutes until it is smooth and elastic. If it is still a bit sticky, add some more flour.

Divide the dough in two batches, one a little bigger than the other. Roll out both batches with a rolling pin until they are about 0.2 inch thick. Sprinkle some flour on the dough so it does not stick to the rolling pin. Place some baking paper on a baking sheet. Place the larger dough layer on the baking sheet. This is the bottom of the empanada. Cut off the excess dough. Distribute the filling evenly over this bottom dough layer, leaving the edges free. Slice the boiled eggs and place the slices on top of the filling. Place the other dough layer on top of the filling. Cut off the excess dough.

Fold the edges of the bottom layer over the top layer and press with your finger or a fork. Prick a small hole in the center of the dough. Whisk the egg yolk and brush it on the top layer of the dough. Bake the empanada for about 35 minutes until the crust is golden.

🍷 A Galician white wine, such as an Albariño or a young red Tempranillo.

¡Gambas a la plancha!
— Grilled shrimp —

Although shrimp might seem like an expensive ingredient, it doesn't have to be. Shrimp are usually available in different price categories, fresh or frozen.

In Spain I always buy them fresh since they are available everywhere, even most supermarkets have their own fish section. In Holland frozen shrimp are usually cheaper and I always have a bag in the freezer. I usually buy the large kind, the tiger prawns which have the black lines across their backs, like a tiger.
Raw shrimp are grey but once grilled they turn pink or red. They are done when the color stops changing. Don't overcook, they will turn dry and tough. Eat them with your hands, you will wind up licking your fingers.

Serves 4

olive oil
1 lb/500 large shrimp
1 tbsp coarse sea salt
parsley-garlic oil
(see recipe on page 168)

Heat a grill pan (with ridges) over high heat and pour in just enough olive oil so that the bottom is covered. When the oil is hot, place the shrimp in the pan with all the heads facing one side. Sprinkle with ½ tbsp salt and drizzle generously with the parsley oil. Grill the shrimp for about 5 minutes and turn. Sprinkle with the remaining salt and drizzle with the parsley-oil.
Grill for about 3 more minutes, drizzle with some more parsley-garlic oil and serve at once.

Serving suggestion: *Gambas a la plancha* are delicious on top of paella (see recipe on page 81) or arroz negro (see recipe on page 154). Prepare them while the rice is 'resting'.

🍷 A nice Albariño with a salty tang.

¡Zarzuela!
— Spanish fish stew —

La Zarzuela is the official residence of the King of Spain. It is also the place where *Zarzuelas*, typical Spanish operettas which combine spoken and sung scenes, used to be performed. Zarzuela, the dish, is also a combination of sorts, mixing all kinds of culinary delights. First you have to prepare a picada, a typical Spanish bread and nut 'sauce', which is used as a thickener for the zarzuela but also adds flavor. Thickening sauces with bread or nuts is an ancient Spanish cooking technique, which was used even before the Middles Ages. People often ask me for an easy Zarzuela recipe. Here goes!

Serves 4

-Picada-
2 tbsp olive oil
1 slice/40 g white bread
1 garlic clove
¼ tsp salt
3 tbsp/30 g roasted almonds
2–3 sprigs of flat-leaf parsley

-Zarzuela-
14 oz/400 g of white fish (cod, hake, mullet or monkfish)
salt
all-purpose flour
4 tbsp olive oil
8 large shrimp or langoustines
coarse sea salt
1 onion
3 garlic cloves
2 tomatoes
9 oz/250 g squid, cut in rings
1 pinch of saffron threads
1–2 tsp smoked paprika
1 cup/200 ml fish stock
¼ cup/50 ml white wine
16 mussels
9 oz/250 g clams
flat-leaf parsley

optional:
1–2 tbsp Spanish Brandy
1 dried chili pepper

Heat the olive oil in a sauté pan. Sauté the bread over medium-high heat until crunchy. Using a mortar and pestle, grind the bread with the almonds, garlic and parsley.

Sprinkle the fish with salt and lightly dust with flour. Heat 1 tbsp of olive oil in a large skillet and sauté the fish for 30–60 seconds on each side. Remove the fish from the pan and set aside. In the same pan, sauté the shrimp with coarse sea salt for 1–2 minutes on each side. (Optional step: Pour a shot of Brandy and flambé the shrimp) Remove the shrimp from the pan and set aside. Finely chop the onion, garlic and the tomatoes. Pour 2 tbsp of olive oil in the same pan and sauté the onion and garlic (and the chili pepper if you like a bit more heat) for 5–8 minutes. Add the squid and sauté for about 2 minutes over medium-high heat. Add the tomato, saffron and smoked paprika. (optional step: Deglaze with 1–2 tbsp Brandy)
Pour in the fish stock and white wine. Slowly bring to a boil.
Meanwhile, add an inch or so of water to the bottom of a different pot, add some salt and steam the mussels for about 1 minute until they open. In another skillet, heat 1 tbsp of olive oil and sauté the clams for 1 minute until they open.

Add the fish, shrimp, the mussels and clams to the pan with the squid in the sauce and gently stir in the picada. Cook for 5 minutes over low heat. Garnish with the flat-leaf parsley.

Serving suggestion: Serve the Zarzuela in a decorative Spanish-style clay pot

🍷 A dry white Rueda Verdejo.

¡Lubina a la sal aromatizada!
— Seabass baked in herbed salt crust —

Baking fish in a salt crust is one of the world's oldest cooking techniques. In Spain it is mainly used in the regions near the Mediterranean, where there are many salt flats (*salinas*). This classic way of preparing fish seems difficult but is actually quite easy and always very impressive. The fish cooks in its own juices inside the crust which makes it come out wonderfully moist and delicious. By adding herbs and spices to the salt you can give this dish a bit of an exotic touch.

Serves 2-4

1 handful of flat-leaf parsley
1 tbsp pink or mixed peppercorns
2 lemons
2 lbs/1 kg coarse sea salt
½ cup/100 ml water
1 whole seabass (about 1 lb/500 g) (cleaned but not descaled, the scales prevent the salt from being absorbed through the skin)
2 garlic cloves

Preheat the oven to 400°F/200°C. Finely chop 2/3 of the parsley, crush the peppercorns and zest the lemon. Mix it all with the salt and add water until it forms a thick paste.
Rinse and dry the fish. Finely slice one the of the lemons, flatten and chop the garlic. Finely chop the remaining parsley. Combine the lemon, garlic and parsley, then stuff the belly of the fish with this mixture.
Line a baking tray with parchment paper and spread half of the salt paste out over the bottom. Place the fish on top of the salt layer and spoon the rest of the salt paste over the fish. Don't cover the head and the tail. Using your hands, shape the salt paste into a cocoon around the body of the fish. Place the tray in the oven and bake for exactly 31 minutes. (My fishmonger in Spain swears by this method. Another way of telling whether the fish is cooked, is when its eyes are opaque instead of translucent.) Remove the tray from the oven but leave the fish on the tray. Tap the salt crust with a rolling pin until it cracks and carefully remove it. Fillet the fish and serve with parsley-garlic oil (see recipe on page 168).

Serving suggestion: Serve with a salad.

Exotic variations for the salt crust:
-add ½ tsp smoked paprika and/or Sichuan pepper to the salt
-add 1 tbsp aniseed or fennel seed to the salt
-substitute the lemon with lime
-substitute the parsley with cilantro or dill

🍷 A Rueda Superior.

… # ¡Gambas al ajillo!
— Garlic shrimp —

You really need to use a Spanish-style clay pot to prepare these garlic shrimp. The clay retains the heat for a long time so you will hear the shrimp sizzle in the wonderfully aromatic garlic and chili oil. The sauce is as tasty as the shrimp, if not more. Make sure you have enough bread available for dipping.

Serves 3–4

- 9 oz/250 g peeled (frozen) shrimp
- 4 garlic cloves
- 1 spring onion
- 1–2 dried chili peppers
- ¼ cup/50 ml olive oil
- salt
- 1/8 cup/25 ml Pedro Ximénez, Sherry or white wine
- grated zest of 1 lemon

When using frozen shrimp, defrost first. Cut the garlic, the spring onion and chili pepper into thin slices. Heat the olive oil in clay pot over high heat. When the oil begins to smoke, add the slices of garlic and chili pepper. Mix together and add the shrimp before the garlic starts to color. Sauté for 2 minutes over high heat. Add the Sherry or white wine and spring onion. Cover the pot, remove from heat and place on the table. You should still hear the shrimp sizzle.

🍷 A nice tangy Albariño or a full-bodied Rueda superior/Centenario.

¡Trio de mejillones!
— Mussel Trio —

Three mussel dishes for every taste: spicy, crisp and creamy.

Serves 4

-Mejillones con salsa brava-
2 lbs/1 kg mussels
¼ cup/50 ml dry white wine (such as Albariño)
¼ cup/50 ml water
2 bay leaves
salt

-Salsa brava-
2/3 cup/100 g onion
2–3 tbsp olive oil
Salt
1/3 cup/40 g flour
1–2 tbsp smoked paprika (sweet)
1–2 tbsp smoked paprika (spicy)
2 cups/500 ml mussel broth
Optional: 2 cups/500 ml fish stock or broth

-Mejillones en escabeche-
2 lbs/1 kg mussels
¼ cup/50 ml white wine
salt
1 bay leaf

-Marinade-
1 onion
2 garlic cloves
4 tbsp extra virgin olive oil
salt
black pepper
1 bay leaf
½–1 tsp smoked paprika
2 tbsp spring onion
2 tbsp Sherry vinegar

-Mejillones con salsa de azafrán-
1 onion
2 garlic cloves
2 tbsp olive oil
1 pinch of saffron (threads)
½ cup/100 ml white wine
½ cup/100 ml heavy cream
salt
black pepper
2 lbs/1 kg mussels
2 tbsp flat-leaf parsley

Mejillones con salsa brava - mussels in salsa brava
Place the mussels in a bowl filled with water, discard the ones that are open and the ones that are damaged. Place the mussels in a pan and add the wine, water, bay leaves and a pinch of salt. Bring to a boil until the mussels open. This will take a few minutes. Remove from the heat so they don't overcook and dry out. Discard any mussels that do not open. Save the broth. Pull the mussels from the shell, place them on a platter and keep warm. Prepare the salsa brava, pour over the mussels and serve at once.

Everyone is familiar with salsa brava from the tapa with the sautéed potatoes, however, in Ponferrada, my grandmother's town, they also serve it with mussels. Not just any salsa brava, possibly the most delicious salsa brava in all of Spain. The special ingredient in this salsa brava is the broth in which you have cooked the mussels. A remarkable but delicious combination. The actual recipe is a closely held secret, but I think I get close in my version.

Dice the onion. Heat the olive oil in a skillet over medium-high heat and sauté the onion with a pinch of salt for about 5 minutes until soft. Add the flour and cook for another minute. Keep stirring. Add both kinds of smoked paprika and pour in a bit of the mussel broth. You need about 2 cups of broth for this sauce. If you don't have enough broth, add some fish stock. Bring to a low boil and keep stirring for about 10 minutes until the sauce thickens.

Mejillones en escabeche - marinated mussels
Prepare the mussels in the same way as above but take note of the different ingredients. After they mussels are cooked, remove from the pan and allow to cool.

Marinade
Finely slice the onion and the garlic. Heat the olive oil in a skillet and sauté the onion and garlic, together with a pinch of salt and pepper, for about 5 minutes over medium-high heat. Add the bay leaf, the smoked paprika and the spring onion. Mix well and transfer to a bowl.
Transfer the mussels and the broth to the same bowl and add the Sherry vinegar. Mix well and place the bowl in the refrigerator and let the mussels marinate for 4 hours or more.

Mejillones con salsa de azafrán - mussels with a saffron cream sauce
Finely dice the onion and the garlic. Heat the olive oil in a skillet and sauté the onion and the garlic for about 5 minutes over low to medium-high heat until translucent. Add the saffron and the wine and bring to a boil. Let the sauce boil down to about half the amount and puree with an immersion blender. Add the cream and season with salt and pepper.
Clean the mussels (see first recipe) and add to the sauce and mix well. Cover the pan and cook for about 5–7 minutes until the mussels have opened. Chop the parsley and sprinkle over the mussels before serving.

🍷 A dry white wine such as a Rueda Verdejo.

¡Chipirones rellenos en su tinta!
— Stuffed squid in ink sauce —

In the mood for something special? How about trying to cook something with squid ink.
For Spanish people this is quite normal but in most other countries you will definitely impress your dinner guests. The ink will give your dishes a spectacular color. The flavor is not overpowering, but it does add a special touch which makes any dish extraordinarily delicious. It has a hint of sweetness without being overly sweet when used in combination with other deep, round flavors. The taste is very subtle, the actual flavor is hard to pinpoint. You only need a tiny bit of ink for that special touch. I buy the squid ink packets at a wholesaler or at my fishmonger. Now you can also order it online. It's not expensive and keeps for a long time.

My husband Daniel often has to travel to Spain for work and while there, he has many business lunches and dinners. One time he had to travel to Bilbao and I made him promise to order this dish. In between his business meetings, he tried to coax the waiter to give him the recipe. He managed quite well.

When I prepare this typical Basque dish, I take my time and make a large batch. Cleaning the squid it the most time-consuming part. I like to do this while listening to some Marvin Gaye or Kanye West. Don't ask me why, but their music makes this tedious job a lot more fun.
Look online for tutorials on how to clean the squid.

I usually prepare this dish a day in advance to allow the flavors to blend and to allow the sauce to develop a velvety texture. Be sure to use red onion.

Serves 4

2 lbs/1 kg (frozen) squid (approximately 20, about 5"/12 cm long)
1 lbs/550 g red onion
2–3 garlic cloves
1 green bell pepper
1–2 small tomatoes
18 tbsp olive oil
½ cup/100 ml white wine
1 ½ cup/300 ml water
4 packets squid ink (4g each)
½ cup/100 ml Spanish Brandy or Cognac
Salt

Defrost the squid (if needed) and clean as follows: pull the head, the tentacles and intestines carefully out of the body(mantle) of squid. Try to pull it all out at once. Cut the tentacles from the head, right under the eyes. Stick your finger inside the body and remove the cuttlebone (a piece of cartilage that looks like plastic). Squeeze the body to remove any remaining innards. Remove the purple skin from the body. Rinse the body and the tentacles under running water and pat dry.
Finely chop the onion, garlic, bell pepper and tomatoes.

For the stuffing, chop the tentacles and the wings of the body as finely as possible.
Heat 10 tbsp olive oil in a heavy skillet and sauté half of the chopped onion with a pinch of salt for about 8–10 minutes over medium-high heat until caramelized. Turn up the heat and add the chopped tentacles and wings and an extra pinch of salt. Cook for another 10–15 minutes until the liquid has evaporated. Remove from heat and allow to cool.

For the sauce, heat 8 tbsp of olive oil in another pan and sauté the remaining onions, bell pepper and garlic with a pinch of salt for 8–10 minutes over medium-high heat. Add the wine, let it cook for a bit and add the chopped tomato and the squid ink. Mix well. Add the water and let it simmer for 15–20 minutes over low heat. Puree the sauce and season with salt.

Stuff the squid bodies with the stuffing using a teaspoon or a piping bag. Stuff them half full and secure the wide end of the squid body with a toothpick. Heat 1 tbsp olive oil with a pinch of salt in a skillet and sauté the stuffed squid 5 at a time for about 30 seconds on each side. Remove the squid from the pan. Turn up the heat and deglaze with some Brandy or Cognac. Do the same with the rest of the stuffed squid. Each time after sautéing 5 stuffed squid, deglaze with some Brandy or Cognac. After all the squid has been sautéed, add the sauce to the pan, transfer all the squid back to the pan, cover and cook for about 15 minutes over medium-high heat.

Serving suggestion:
-garnish with some chopped flat-leaf parsley or chives
-serve as a tapa or an appetizer
-serve as a main course with white rice or a mash (see recipes on page 158)

Variations:
-if you prefer a thicker sauce, add some bread to the sauce before pureeing
-add a pinch of cinnamon to the sauce.

Variation for when you are in a lazy mood (the Basque do this as well!)
Buy clean (frozen) squid and defrost before using. Halve the squid and prepare them just as in the recipe above but do not stuff them. Mix the stuffing in the pureed sauce but only use half of the onion.

A dry white wine such as a Rueda, a crisp white Txakoli or a dry Rosado (Spanish rosé).

¡Ensalada de naranja sanguina invernal!
— Winter salad with blood orange —

I simply love this salad. Even the name is mysterious and exciting. The subtle dash of cocoa in the dressing adds an extra dimension to this colorful salad. You don't quite taste it which makes it so much more exciting. This salad will spice up any boring wintery day.

Serves 4

-Dressing-
salt
1 tbsp/15 ml Sherry vinegar
¼ cup/50 ml olive oil
1/8 cup/20 g peeled hazelnuts
½ tsp orange blossom water
1 tsp cocoa or cacao
¼ tsp smoked paprika

-Salad-
1 blood orange
1 head of white or red endive
1 red onion
½ head of fennel
5 radishes
3.5 oz/100 g arugula
2 tbsp pitted black olives
salt or Iberian salt
smoked paprika

optional: chili flakes

Dissolve a pinch of salt in the vinegar and add the olive oil. Stir well until combined. Finely chop the hazelnuts. Add the orange blossom water, the cocoa, the smoked paprika and the chopped hazelnuts to the dressing.

Peel the orange, removing the white pith as well. Cut it into thin slices. Trim the base of the endive, cut in half and remove the core. Peel off the leaves, rinse and dry. Cut the onion, the fennel and the radish into very thin slices. Arrange the fennel slices in a circle around the dish alternating with the endive, spread the arugula out from the center and top with orange slices and radish. Drizzle with the dressing and finish off with the olives, a small pinch of salt and a pinch of smoked paprika. If you like an extra kick, add some chili flakes.

🍷 A crisp white wine such as a Rueda.

¡Sandía a la plancha con ensalada de tomate!
— Grilled watermelon with tomato salad —

Grilling watermelon caramelizes the sugars in the fruit, which will make it sweeter and enhance the flavor in general. It also changes the structure of the watermelon. Most of the fruit's water evaporates leaving you with a firm meaty steak not unlike a tuna steak. I swear it's not like anything you've ever tasted before. Surprise your family and friends with this extraordinary salad.

Serves 4

14 oz/400 g cherry tomatoes
¼ cup/25 g pitted black olives
salt
black pepper
4 tbsp balsamic vinegar
4 tbsp olive oil, plus extra for spreading
1 watermelon
fresh or dried oregano

Halve the cherry tomatoes, chop the olives and place both in a bowl. Pour in the olive oil and vinegar and season with salt and pepper. Mix well and leave to marinate for about 20 minutes. Meanwhile, halve the watermelon and cut into 1-inch-thick slices. Cut these into 4 rectangular 'steaks'. Spread some olive oil on all four steaks. Place a (ridged) grill pan over high heat and grill for about 2–3 minutes on each side until you see grill lines. Allow the steaks to cool. Divide the tomato-olive mixture over the four steaks and drizzle with the marinade. Garnish with a bit of oregano.

Variations:
- Use smoked salt instead of regular salt
- Serve with fresh goat cheese
- Mix a few drops of smoked olive oil into the olive oil you use for brushing the watermelon steaks before grilling.

🍷 A white Rioja or Terra Alta.

¡Ensalada ibérica con melón caramelizado!
— Iberian salad with caramelized melon —

This salad with a Spanish temperament falls into the comfort food category as far as I'm concerned. You can't count calories when you are eating a salad. It just has to taste good. Just like this wonderful combination of ingredients with different textures and temperatures. Don't skimp on the dressing.

Serves 4

-Honey-garlic dressing-
½–1 garlic clove
2 tbsp (Sherry) vinegar
salt
6 tbsp olive oil
3 tbsp honey
Iberian salt (see recipe on page 174)

-Salad-
1.5 oz/40 g Serrano ham
½ melon
10 cherry tomatoes
50 walnuts
5 oz/150 g mixed greens
16 pitted black olives
1–2 tbsp olive oil
salt
black pepper
2–3 tbsp Pedro Ximénez Sherry

Puree the garlic and mix with a pinch of salt and the Sherry vinegar. Slowly add the olive oil until emulsified. Pour in the honey, mix well and season with Iberian salt.

Variation: Substitute the Iberian salt with a pinch of smoked paprika and a pinch of sea salt.

Place the slices of Serrano ham between two sheets of parchment paper and zap in the microwave for a few minutes until crispy. Using a melon baller, scoop out 25 melon balls. Halve the tomatoes and chop the walnuts. Place the mixed greens in a large bowl and add the ham, the tomatoes and the walnuts. Drizzle with the dressing. Heat the olive oil in a heavy skillet and sauté the melon balls with a pinch of salt and pepper for about 5 minutes over medium-high heat. Deglaze with the Pedro Ximénez and cook for another 1–2 minutes. Divide the melon balls over the salad and serve at once.

Variation: Substitute the Serrano ham with Manchego cheese

A Rosado (rosé) from Castile.

¡Ensalada de salpicón de mariscos!
— Seafood salad —

Sometimes you have to prepare something festive at the last minute. Make sure you always have a bag of frozen shellfish in your freezer. With a bit of luck, you will also have an onion and a bell pepper lying around. Garlic and olive oil are a given. Last but not least, a cocktail glass would be nice as well to serve this delicious, colorful and healthy cocktail of seafood and raw vegetables.

Originally, a *salpicón* was made with diced bits of meat served with an onion vinaigrette. This dish even appears in *Don Quixote*, the classic book of Spanish Literature. Nowadays, a *salpicon* is better known as a marriage between the harvest from the sea and from the vegetable garden.

Serves 4

-Dressing-
½ garlic clove
6 tbsp extra virgin olive oil
3 tbsp (Sherry) vinegar
salt
black pepper

-Seafood-
1 lb/500 g frozen shellfish (pre-cooked)
3 tbps olive oil
salt
black pepper
½ red bell pepper
½ green bell pepper
½ red onion
½ fennel bulb
2 tbsp pitted black olives

Puree the garlic, add the olive oil and vinegar and stir well until combined. Season with salt and pepper.

Defrost the shellfish. Heat the olive oil in a skillet and sauté the shellfish for about 2–3 minutes over high heat. Remove from the pan and strain so the shellfish is still a bit firm. Season with salt and pepper. Dice the bell peppers very finely, brunoise style. Slice the onion and fennel into very fine strips, julienne style. Mix all the ingredients together in a bowl and add in the dressing. Place the bowl in the refrigerator for about two hours in order for the flavors to blend.

Vegetarian variety: Substitute the shellfish with 1 lb of cooked chickpeas (from a can). Drain and rinse under running water.

An elegant Albariño.

¡Espárragos verdes a la plancha!
— Grilled asparagus —

There are many ways to prepare asparagus. I always go for the easiest and quickest one, the way they are usually prepared in Spain with only three ingredients. It is a simple and pure recipe.

Serves 4

16 asparagus spears
olive oil
coarse sea salt

Cut the ends off the asparagus and brush the spears with olive oil. Heat 1–2 tbsp olive oil with a pinch of sea salt in a skillet or grill pan with ridges. Sauté the asparagus for about 10-15 minutes over medium-high heat turning regularly. They should still be al dente. Turn off the heat and let them rest in the pan for a few minutes. Place on a plate and drizzle with olive oil and sprinkle with salt.

Serving suggestion: Serve with Serrano ham and/or Manchego cheese. Also good with salsa romesco (see recipe on page 176).

A dry Rueda Sauvignon.

¡Ensalada escalivada!
— Roasted vegetable salad —

Traditionally, the vegetables for this salad were roasted over an open fire, giving them a wonderful smoky flavor. Since an open fire is not very practical, I recommend roasting the vegetables in the oven and then seasoning them with smoked salt and a few drops of smoked olive oil. Escalivada can also be served as a side dish with fish, meat or a green salad.

Serves 4

1 red onion
3 red bell peppers
1 eggplant
olive oil
coarse sea salt
black pepper

Optional:
smoked salt
smoked olive oil

Preheat the oven to 425°F/220°C. Brush the peppers, eggplant and onion with olive oil. Pierce the peppers and the eggplants a few times with a fork to prevent them from bursting in the oven. Place all the vegetables them on a baking sheet and roast for about 30 minutes until they are cooked. Remove from the oven and allow to cool. Remove the skin and the seeds from the pepper and the eggplant. Cut all the vegetables into thin strips and place them in a bowl. Sprinkle with (smoked) salt and drizzle with (smoked) olive oil. Serve with a roasted red pepper cream sauce. (see below)

Serving suggestion:
-Use a ring mold to serve the salad to give it an extra festive look.
-garnish the salad with some mixed olives, some anchovies and/or a (soft) boiled egg

🍷 A full-bodied white wine such as a Chardonnay or a Rueda Centenario.

¡Salsa de pimientos asados con nata!
— Roasted bell pepper cream sauce —

This secret of this very popular sauce is its simplicity. It doesn't involve complicated instructions or expensive ingredients. There is only one downside; chances are the sauce will be finished even before it makes it to the dinner table. For this reason, I always have jars of roasted bell peppers and cream in my kitchen cupboard. This way, I can always liven up any dish or tapas with this very colorful sauce in no time at all. The sauce is delicious with meat, fish, potato and rice dishes, vegetables or bread.

Serves 4

1 garlic clove
3 tbsp olive oil
1 jar roasted red bell peppers
(12oz/350 g drained net weight)
½ tsp salt
½ tsp black pepper
¼ cup/50 ml heavy ream

Optional:
1–2 tsp Spanish Brandy

Finely slice the garlic. Heat 2 tbsp olive oil in a heavy skillet and sauté the garlic for about 2 minutes until golden. Add the roasted bell peppers with the liquid, salt and pepper. Sauté for about 5 minutes over medium-high heat until most of the liquid has evaporated. Put the peppers in a blender, add the cream and 1 tbsp olive oil. Blend until smooth. If you like to jazz it up, add some Spanish Brandy. Serve cool because this is the way the sauce tastes best.

¡Ensalada de habas mixtas!
— Smoky bean salad —

This salad is very Spanish not just because of the smoky pimentón dressing but also because it is quick and easy to prepare and obviously delicious. To me, it just screams Spain!
The velvety lima beans combined with the crunchy sugar snaps and the tart pomegranate seeds make this salad a delight of dueling textures. And did I mention that it is healthy as well?

Serves 2–4

-Smoked paprika-honey dressing-
salt
1 tbsp/15 ml (Sherry) vinegar
3 tbsp/50 ml olive oil
1 garlic clove
1 tsp honey
¼– ½ tsp smoked paprika

-Salad-
5 oz/150 g lima beans (from a can or jar)
5 oz/150 g haricots verts or string beans
5 oz/150 g sugar snaps
¼ cup/25 g shaved almonds
salt
pepper
½ cup 50 g pomegranate seeds

Dissolve a pinch of salt in the vinegar and stir in the olive oil until smooth. Crush the garlic and add to the dressing. Stir in the honey and the smoked paprika

Drain the lima beans. Bring a large pot of salted water to a boil and blanch the string beans and the sugar snaps for 2 minutes. Drain and then cool in ice water so the vegetables stay crunchy. Dry roast the almonds for a few seconds, making sure they don't burn.

Carefully toss the lima beans with string beans and sugar snaps and season with salt and pepper. Dress with the smoked paprika-honey dressing and garnish with the roast almonds and the pomegranate seeds.

🍷 A light red wine, such as a Rioja Joven or a dry Rosado (Spanish rosé).

¡Puerros caramelizados con salsa romesco!
— Caramelized leeks with romesco sauce —

Salsa romesco is a popular Catalan sauce which is traditionally served with *calçots* which is a type of large spring onion. Since this is only available in Catalonia, I prepare this dish with leeks. The sauce is also delicious with meat, fish, grilled vegetables or as a dip with bread.

Serves 4

10 oz/300 g leeks
1 tbsp olive oil
1 tbsp butter
½ tbsp sugar
salt
black pepper
romesco sauce (see recipe on page 176)

Cut the leeks into pieces of about 3 inches each. Heat the olive oil and the butter in a heavy skillet and add the sugar. Sear the leeks with a dash of salt and pepper for about 1–2 minutes over high heat. Lower the heat and sauté for another 10 minutes until the leeks are caramelized. Serve the leeks with the romesco sauce.

A white wine from Galicia, such as an Albariño.

¡Garbanzos crujientes con espinacas!
— Crunchy chickpeas with spinach —

This recipe is my own take on one of the traditional Spanish Lenten dishes, chickpeas with spinach and salted cod. Lent is the Catholic commemoration of the suffering of Jesus Christ. This 40-day period starts the day after Carnival and ends with Easter. During this these weeks, Catholics reflect on the 40 days Jesus spent in the desert and they fast. Or rather, they abstain from eating certain foods. For instance, no meat on Fridays. I am afraid I am not a good Catholic since I like to make this dish with chorizo. It would seem that Jesus Christ was a bit more flexible than his father, since he didn't make his disciples fast. Maybe he wouldn't have minded the chorizo. The *potage de vigilia* (Lenten stew) was traditionally prepared with the staples that were available in every Spanish pantry: salted cod, pulses and some vegetables. Nowadays, the dish has become a popular tapa just like many other traditional Lenten dishes.

Serves 4

-Crunchy chickpeas-
3 oz/50–100 g dried salted cod
1 can of chickpeas
(drained net weight 13.40 oz/380 g)
2 tbsp olive oil
½ tsp salt
½ tsp black pepper
½ tsp cumin seed
¼ tsp cinnamon
½ tsp smoked paprika
2–4 tbsp flat-leaf parsley
grated zest and juice of ½ lime

Optional:
50 g chorizo

-Sautéed spinach-
2 tbsp olive oil
2/3 cup/150 g fresh spinach
2 tbsp pine nuts
2 tbsp raisins
salt
pepper
smoked paprika

Soak the salted cod according to the instructions on the package. (This process can take hours). Drain the chickpeas. Chop the chorizo into pieces that are smaller than the chickpeas. Heat the olive oil in a heavy pan and add the chickpeas. Sauté over high heat with some salt and pepper while shaking the pan gently back and forth. After two minutes, add the cumin, the cinnamon, the smoked paprika and the cod. Keep shaking the pan. Lower the heat and sauté for another 10 minutes until the chickpeas, the cod and the chorizo are crunchy. In the meantime, chop the parsley and add this at the last minute. Drizzle with olive oil, lemon juice and lemon zest. Remove the mixture from the pan and keep it warm.

In the same pan, heat 2 tbsp olive oil and sauté the spinach with the pine nuts and raisins or 2–3 minutes over medium-high heat until the spinach is wilted. Season with salt, pepper and smoked paprika. Mix with the chickpeas, cod and chorizo.

Serving suggestions: Place a soft-boiled egg on top or serve with toasted bread with goat cheese.

Vegetarian option: Leave out the cod and chorizo and add 1 tsp or oregano and an additional ½ tsp smoked paprika.

A full bodied white wine such as a Chardonnay or a blend with Xarel·lo.

¡Morcilla vegetariana!
— Vegetarian blood sausage —

Blood sausage tastes much better than it sounds. I prefer to call it by its Spanish name, *morcilla* which is just a much nicer word. Morcilla is an integral part of Spanish cuisine and you will find it on the menu in many tapas bars and restaurants. If you are a vegetarian or just want a meat-free meal for a change, black beans are a healthy alternative. This recipe is inspired by the morcilla de Burgos which is made with rice.

Makes 16 tapas

- ¼ cup/45 g white rice (short grain)
- 5 oz/150 g canned black beans
- ½ onion
- olive oil
- salt
- ¾ cup/40 g bread crumbs
- 2 tsp dried oregano
- ½ tsp cumin
- ¼ tsp cinnamon
- ½ tsp smoked paprika
- 1-2 tsp garlic powder
- ½ tsp black pepper
- ¼ cup/50 g flour
- 2 apples
- butter
- 3–4 tbsp Pedro Ximénez Sherry

Boil the rice in plenty of salted water for about 20 minutes. Drain the beans but collect the liquid. Puree the beans, adding 1–2 tbsp of the bean liquid until you have a smooth paste. Reserve the remaining liquid. Dice and sauté the onions in 1 tbsp olive oil with a pinch of salt for about 5 minutes over low heat. First mix the pureed beans with the boiled rice, then add the sautéed onions, the spices, and the bread crumbs. Season with salt and pepper. Add the flour and knead into a dough. If it is too dry, add some more of the bean liquid. If it is too wet, add some more flour. It should be a soft mass but should not stick to your hands. Divide the dough in two batches and make two 6-inch diameter rolls. Take two large pieces of heat-resistant plastic wrap and wrap each roll 3 or 4 times tightly with the plastic wrap. Make a knot on both ends. Place a large pot of water on the stove and gently boil the rolls for about 30 minutes over low to medium-high heat. Remove the rolls from the pan and allow to cool. Remove the plastic wrap. Cut into ½ inch slices. Heat a 2 tbsp olive oil per sausage in a heavy skillet and sauté each slice for 4-5 minutes per side until crunchy from the outside but still juicy on the inside. Turn up the heat and sauté for another minute per side to make them extra crunchy. Dust each slice with a pinch of smoked paprika. Peel the apples and cut into thin slices. Heat one tbsp butter in a skillet and sauté the apple slices for about 5 minutes until golden brown. Deglaze with the Pedro Ximénez. Serve the morcilla with the caramelized apple slices.

Serving suggestion:
- Make a morcilla tapa by taking a piece of toasted white bread or pan con tomate (see recipe on page 38) add some caramelized apple slices and top with a slice of morcilla.
- If you want to go all out, add a fried quail egg, a few strips of roasted bell pepper and a pinch of smoked paprika. Drizzle with roasted pepper cream sauce (see recipe on page 124).
- Very good with the mixed bean salad (see recipe on page 128).

For carnivores: This tapa is also very tasty with real blood sausage.

🍷 A red wine with character such as a Mencia from the Bierzo region.

¡Paella vegetal!
— Vegetarian paella —

My most traumatic moment in the kitchen occurred when I was participating in MasterChef Holland in 2015. The assignment was to prepare a dish with mini vegetables. I thought I would steal the show with a delicious vegetarian paella but in a momentary lapse of reason I added a whole can of tomato paste to the rice. It made for a paella and a departure from MasterChef that were equally bitter. To get over this trauma, I decided to come up with the ultimate vegetarian paella. I think I succeeded since not only do my vegetarian friends love this dish but my carnivore friends do too.

Serves 3–4

pinch of saffron (10–20 threads)
2–3 garlic cloves
½ eggplant
1 red bell pepper
3,5 oz/100 g flat beans
1 tomato
4 oz/125 g mixed mushrooms shitake, oyster, button mushrooms etc.
4 oz /125 g artichoke hearts from a jar (drained)
1/3 cup/75 ml olive oil
salt
½ tsp thyme
½ tsp rosemary
½ tsp smoked paprika
1 packet paella seasoning (3 g)
3 cups/650 ml hot water (note: proportions differ from the paella Valenciana)
1 bay leaf
1 tbsp/5 g wakame, (dried) seaweed
2/3 cup/150 g paella rice
3 sprigs fresh rosemary

Mix the saffron with 2 tbsp of water and heat this for 20 seconds in the microwave. This will intensify the flavor and the color. Flatten and crush the garlic and dice the eggplant (2-inch cubes). Dice the bell pepper (1/2-inch pieces) Slice or break the runner beans (1-inch pieces). Cut the tomatoes into very small pieces. Dice the artichoke hearts (1-inch cubes). Heat the oil in a paella pan or a large sauté pan over low to medium-high heat with a pinch of salt to prevent spattering. Sauté the garlic for about 2 minutes until it starts to color. In the same pan, sauté the runner beans and the tomato for about 2 minutes over medium-high heat. Add the rest of the vegetables and sauté for another 8–10 minutes over medium-high heat. The juice of the tomato will prevent the garlic from burning. Add the thyme, rosemary, smoked paprika, and the paella seasoning. Carefully mix together. Pour in the hot water and add the bay leaf and cook for 5 minutes over low heat. Taste and season with salt. Add the saffron. Add the rice and the wakame and mix together carefully. Cook for 10 minutes over medium to high heat. Lower the heat and let the rice cook for 10 minutes more. Place the rosemary sprigs on top. Do not stir! It is important that all the water has evaporated by the time the rice has reached the al dente cooking point. The rice kernels should feel dry and loose. In order to get an extra crispy crust (socarrat) at the bottom of the pan, pour one tbsp of olive oil over the rice. Turn up the heat for one minute. The oil will sink to the bottom of the pan allowing the rice to get a little 'fried'. Turn off the heat and cover the paella with a newspaper. Let it rest for a few minutes. Serve with saffron aioli (see recipe on page 166) and a few lemon slices.

Variation: Roast a few mini vegetables such as broccoli, asparagus, bell peppers, (purple) cauliflower, and place these on top of the paella.

A full-bodied white wine such as a Chardonnay from Penedès or a Rueda Superior or Centenario. For those who prefer a red, a light Tempranillo such a as a Rioja Joven or Crianza.

¡Bocadillo de tinta de calamares!
— Squid ink bun with calamari —

During my student years in Madrid I cured many hangovers with a *bocadillo de calamares*. It is the quintessential snack of Madrid, a crispy baguette with fried squid. In those days, it was a delicious treat and a great cure for only 50 cents. A quarter century later in Barcelona, the hangover was caused by the bill I was presented for a mini bocadillo de calamares. It was tiny but I couldn't resist the temptation since the bun looked so delicious. It was completely black with white specks (sesame seeds). Combined with the white mayonnaise and the golden *calamares*, it was picture perfect and turned out to be delicious and definitely worth the hefty price tag.

Makes 6 burgers

-Squid ink buns-
3 bags of squid ink 4 g each
½ cup/125 ml lukewarm water
1 tbsp olive oil
7 g dry yeast (1 packet)
1 tsp salt
2 cups/250 g flour
sesame seeds

-Lime mayonnaise-
a few drops of lime juice
½ cup/150 g mayonnaise

-Squid rings-
1 lb/500 g frozen squid rings
salt
½ cup/75 g flour
1 cup/250 ml olive oil

-Fried onion rings-
1 onion
1 cup/120 g flour
1 tsp dry yeast
½ tsp salt
1 tsp smoked paprika
½ cup/150 ml ice water
olive oil

Mix the squid ink with the water and the olive oil in a bowl. First add the yeast and then the salt. Bit by bit, add the flour and knead it for a few minutes until the dough feels smooth and elastic. Let the dough rise for 1-2 hours in a warm and dry spot until it is doubled in size. Preheat the oven to 400°F/200 °C. Knead the dough for a few minutes to remove the air bubbles. Shape the dough into 6 balls and place these on a baking sheet. Moisten the tops with a bit of water and then sprinkle with sesame seeds. Bake the buns for about 15 minutes until done.

Add a few drops of lime juice to the mayonnaise. If you want to make the lime mayonnaise from scratch, see recipe on page 72.

Defrost the squid rings and dust with a pinch of salt. Take a plastic bag, pour in the flour and add the squid. Shake the bag until all the squid rings are covered with a layer of flour. Place them in a colander and shake of any excess flour. Heat the olive oil in a heavy skillet and fry the squid rings for about 5 minutes until crunchy on the outside and cooked on the inside. Drain on a paper towel.

Cut the squid ink buns in half, place the squid rings on the bottom half of the bun, drizzle the lime mayonnaise over the squid rings and top with the other half of the bun.

Serving suggestion: Add some lettuce just as you would with a hamburger.

Vegetarian variation: Replace the squid ink with activated charcoal (0,04 oz/ 1,2 g) from a health food store. Replace the squid rings with onion rings.

Slice the onion into thin rings. Mix the flour, yeast, smoked paprika, salt and water in a bowl. Dip the onion rings one by one in the batter. Heat the olive oil in a heavy skillet and fry the onion rings in about 4 minutes over high heat until crunchy. Drain on a paper towel.

Cut the black rolls in half, spread some lime mayonnaise on the bottom half, add a layer of squid rings and cover with the top half of the roll.

🍷 Spanish beer or Rueda wine (Verdejo).

¡Bikini ibérico!
— Iberian grilled sandwich —

I don't like eating in front of the television. I actually hate it, but I'll make an exception for this grilled sandwich. I like to eat it when no one else is home.

This grilled sandwich is very popular in Spanish cafés. The name supposedly comes from the oldest disco in Barcelona, Sala Bikini, where they used to serve them all night long. Also, the sandwich is cut into triangles which actually resemble the classic bikini top.

Makes 4

8 slices of white sandwich bread
butter
aioli (see recipe on page 166)
8 slices Serrano ham
8 slices Manchego cheese
smoked paprika

Optional:
1 small truffle (from a jar)

Spread some butter on the outside of the bread slices and some aioli on the inside. Cover four of the bread slices with 2 slices of Serrano ham followed by 2 slices of Manchego cheese, a pinch of smoked paprika, some grated truffle (optional) and then top them with the remaining four slices of bread with the butter on the outside. Place the sandwich in a panini press and cook until the cheese has melted. You can also prepare the sandwich in a skillet. Melt some butter in a skillet and grill the sandwich for 4–5 minutes per side over low to medium-high heat until the cheese melts and the bread is golden brown and crunchy. Remove from the pan, cut into triangles and serve at once.

Variation for an extra crunchy sandwich: Substitute the butter on the outside with a layer of mayonnaise. You can leave out the aioli.

A young Tempranillo or a Spanish beer.

¡Tortitas de guisantes!
— Green Pea pancakes —

This recipe was inspired by a traditional Spanish dish, *guisantes con jamón* (green peas with ham). Simple, affordable and full of flavor. I associate this dish with the end of a long summer vacation in Spain. Quite often this was the last meal we ate in the Basque country before crossing the Spanish-French border. Fighting back my tears, I would eat guisantes con jamón while thinking about our wonderful vacation which was almost over. In honor of these meals, I came up with this festive version of *guisantes con jamón*.

Makes about 8 pancakes

15 fresh mint leaves
salt
1 ½–2 cups/250 g frozen peas
ice cubes
2 eggs
1–2 tbsp (spelt) flour
¼ tsp baking powder
black pepper
½ tsp powdered aniseed
¼ tsp cinnamon
½ tsp smoked paprika
olive oil
12 quail eggs

Finely chop the mint. Bring a large pot of salted water to a boil and blanch the peas for 1–2 minutes until they are cooked but still al dente. Drain and run under cold water. Take a third of the peas and put them in a bowl with ice water to keep their vibrant green color.
Puree the remaining peas with the eggs into a smooth mixture. If needed, add 1–2 tbsp water. Add the flour, baking powder, salt, pepper, aniseed, cinnamon, smoked paprika, mint leaves and the whole peas and mix carefully. The batter should have the same consistency as pancake batter. Cook the pancakes, 4 at a time using ½ tbsp oil for one tbsp batter. Cook for about 3 minutes on each side over medium to high heat. Flip the pancakes when you see little air bubbles pop in the batter. Place then on a plate and keep warm. Boil the quail eggs for about 2 1/2 minutes, leaving the yolks soft. Divide the quail eggs over the pancakes,

Serving suggestions: Take a few slices of Serrano ham and place them between two sheets of parchment paper. Cook in the microwave at the highest setting for a few minutes until crispy. Place some of the crispy ham on top of the pancakes and finish off with a quail egg and pinch of coarse salt, some pepper or Iberian salt (see recipe on page 174). Delicious with aioli (see recipe on page 166).

A Tempranillo or a Rosado (Spanish rosé).

¡Cupcakes ibéricos!
— Iberian cupcakes —

These savory cupcakes with a Spanish twist are great as an appetizer, with a soup or a salad.

Makes 16

- 1/3 cup/30 g spring onions
- 2 oz/60 g black olives
- 4 eggs
- 1 tsp salt
- 1 ½ cups/200 g flour
- 2-1/2 tsps of dry yeast (7 g)
- 1 tbsp smoked paprika
- ½ cup/100 ml whole milk
- 2/3 cup/150 ml olive oil
- 2 oz/50 g chorizo (Spanish dried a cured sausage)
- 2 oz/50 g Manchego cheese

Preheat the oven to 375°F/190°C. Cut the chorizo into very small pieces. Grate the Manchego. Cut the spring onions and olives into thin slices. Whisk the eggs with the salt. Mix the flour with the yeast, smoked paprika, milk, olive oil, spring onions and the olives. Add the eggs and mix well. Divide the batter over two bowls and add chorizo to one bowl and Manchego to the other one. Mix well. Scoop the chorizo batter into an 8-cup muffin pan and do the same with the Manchego batter. Place the muffin pans in the oven and bake for about 20 minutes.

Variation: Sauté the chorizo for a few minutes before adding it to the batter. It makes for a more intense flavor.

Serving suggestion: Serve with lentil soup or *fabada* (see recipe on page 52).

🍷 Serve with a light Tempranillo, such as a Rioja.

¡Bacalao con toque español!
— Cod with a Spanish twist —

How about giving cod a Spanish makeover by using olive oil, saffron, squid ink and aioli?
It is fun to do and not complicated at all.
Cod is a predator and feeds on crayfish, herring and shrimp. In spite of this refined diet, cod itself actually tastes quite bland. It should be a flavor explosion like pork from the Iberian pig that exclusively eats berries, acorns and herbs. However, it is possible to make this fish into something very special using the confit method. Confit is a cooking method in which meat or fish is cooked very slowly at a low temperature. In this case you are poaching the cod in olive oil, which makes it wonderfully soft, tender and juicy. Use extra virgin olive oil for extra flavor. This is an ideal and easy method for preparing mild fish like cod. Another exciting way of cooking cod is au gratin.

Serves 4

-Squid ink crumble-
1 piece of baguette (2 oz/70 g)
water
1 tbsp olive oil
1 packet squid ink (4 g)
Salt

-Anise flavored potatoes-
4 waxy/new potatoes
2 cups/500 ml fish stock
1 pinch of saffron (5-8 threads)
1 tbsp anise liqueur (Marie Brizard, Pernod)
salt
black pepper

-Cod-
4 cod fillets (5 oz/150 g each)
salt
black pepper
olive oil
4 tbsp aioli (see recipe on page 166)
2 tbsp shaved almonds

Bacalao con aioli gratinado - Cod with aioli au gratin
Preheat the oven to 340°F/170°C. Soak the bread for about 5 minutes in water. Squeeze out the excess water and place in a bowl. Add the olive oil, squid ink and salt and puree until smooth. Line a baking tray with parchment paper and spread the bread pulp on top. Place another sheet of parchment paper on top and flatten with your hands. (The layer should only be 0.10 inch thick). Place the tray in the oven for about 15 minutes until the crumble is crunchy.

Peel and slice the potatoes into 1/2-inch slices. Rinse with water and pat dry. Boil them in the fish stock for about 10 minutes, adding the anise liqueur after 5 minutes. The potatoes should still be al dente. Drain and season with salt and pepper.

Preheat the oven to 350°F/180°C. Line a baking tray or casserole dish with parchment paper. Place the cod in the dish and sprinkle with salt, pepper and olive oil. Place the tray in the oven and roast for 10 minutes. Remove the tray from the oven and turn on the broiler.
Spread 1 tbsp aioli on each fillet and sprinkle some shaved almonds on top. Place the tray under the broiler and broil until the fish and the almonds are golden brown.

Divide the potatoes over 4 plates, place the fish on top and finish off with a bit of the squid ink crumble.

Serving suggestion: Try it with a few drops of parsley-garlic oil (see recipe on page 168).

An easy but robust white wine such as a Rioja or a white wine from Castile.

Serves 4

-Saffron sauce-
Pinch of saffron (4 threads)
1 small onion
¼ garlic clove
1 ¾ tbsp/25 g butter
1 tbsp white Martini
1 cup/250 ml fish stock
Scant 1 cup/200 ml heavy cream
salt
white pepper

-Cauliflower aioli-
1 cup/250 g cauliflower
salt
1 garlic clove
Scant 1 cup/200 ml olive oil
black pepper

-Potato aioli-
3.5 oz/100 g potatoes
½ garlic clove
3 tbsp/50 ml olive oil
1 tbsp milk or heavy cream
salt

-Fried leeks-
1 leek
olive oil
salt

- Cod Confit -
3 cups/750 ml olive oil
1 garlic clove
1 sprig fresh rosemary
1 strip of finely shaved orange skin
1 tsp (mixed) peppercorns
4 cod fillets (5 oz/150 g each) room temperature
smoked paprika
salt
pepper

Bacalao confitado - Cod Confit

Wrap the saffron threads in a piece of tin foil and heat for about 1 minute in a skillet. Finely dice the onion and garlic and sauté in 1 tbsp of butter in a heavy skillet for about 5 minutes over low heat until translucent. Deglaze with the Martini. Add the broth, the cream and the saffron. Cook for about 30 minutes over low to medium high heat until it has reduced by one third. Add the remaining (cold) butter. Season with salt and pepper and mix well.

Break the cauliflower info florets and boil in salted water for about 10 minutes until cooked. Drain and allow to cool. Puree with the garlic in a blender. Slowly pour in the olive oil and blend until smooth. Season with salt and pepper.

Boil the potatoes with the garlic for about 20 minutes until cooked. Puree the potatoes and garlic with a fork or a masher. Slowly add the olive oil while stirring until the mixture has the consistency of mayonnaise. Add the cream or milk and season with salt.

Julienne the leeks. Heat a generous amount of olive oil in a deep skillet to 350°F/180°C. Test by tossing in a piece of bread, if it turns golden brown instantly, the oil is hot enough. Fry the julienned leeks for a few seconds until golden brown and crunchy. Drain on paper towels.

Heat the olive oil with the garlic, rosemary, orange peel and peppercorns in a heavy skillet to 140–150°F/60–65 °C. If possible, do this a day in advance and let the oil sit overnight so all the flavors are absorbed. Heat the flavored oil to 190°F/90°C and place the cod in the pan skin side down. The fillets should be covered by oil. Poach the cod for about 10 minutes. The temperature should remain 190°F/90°C. Once the cod turns opaque, it is cooked.

Spread a layer of cauliflower aioli or potato aioli on a plate and place the cod on top. Drizzle some of the flavored oil on the cod. Season with smoked paprika, salt and pepper. Garnish with the fried leek strips. Serve with the saffron sauce.

🍷 A full-bodied white wine such as a Rueda Superior/Centenario or a Chardonnay.

¡Arroz negro!
— Black rice —

Arroz negro with aioli is one of my all-time favorite dishes. In part because I always eat this dish on the beach in Ibiza, one of my favorite places. Add a glass of chilled Albariño and I am happy. There couldn't be a more perfect setting.

Arroz negro was my signature dish when I competed in MasterChef. I didn't have any expectations when I signed up for the competition. During the first week I jumped at the opportunity to prepare arroz negro when I saw the squid ink in the MasterChef store. The judges loved my rice. I was the winner of the day and thus was guaranteed a spot in the second week of the competition.

Serves 4

-Herb oil-
2 garlic cloves
½ tsp salt
¼ cup/60 ml olive oil
2 tbsp/10 g flat-leaf parsley

-Arroz negro-
1 lb/500 g (frozen) squid
3 garlic cloves
1 tsp tomato paste
10 oz/300 g paella rice
1 cup/250 ml dry white wine
1 cup/250 ml fish stock
½ cup/100 ml water
4 packets squid ink (4 g each)
2 tbsp/10 g wakame (dried seaweed)
aioli
1–2 lemons

Puree all the ingredients for the herb oil until smooth and set aside.

Defrost the squid and cut into 1-inch pieces. Flatten and mince the garlic. Heat the herb oil in a heavy skillet and sauté the squid for 3–7 minutes over medium-high heat until and golden brown and done. Keep stirring. Add the garlic and the tomato paste. Mix well. Add the rice, keep stirring and sauté for a few minutes over medium-high heat. Turn up the heat and add half of the wine. Boil for a minute then lower the heat and let it simmer for about 5 minutes, stirring occasionally. Pour in the rest of the wine. Turn the heat up a bit and let it simmer for another 5 minutes, stirring occasionally. Turn the heat up further and add half the fish stock. Stir well. Lower the heat again and let it reduce for a few minutes. Mix the remaining fish stock with the water and squid ink and then add this mixture to the rice. Gently still in the wakame. Cook for another 12 minutes, stirring occasionally. Turn off the heat and cover the pan with aluminum foil. Let the rice rest for 5 minutes before serving.

Serving suggestion:
-Serve with aioli and lemon wedges
-mix some aioli into the black rice
-serve with gambas a la plancha (see recipe on page 98)

🍷 A white wine with character, such as Albariño or Rueda Superior.

¡Pulpo y chocolate!
— Octopus and Chocolate —

The Maragatos were merchants who were involved in the olive oil and smoked paprika trade in northwestern Spain during the Moorish occupation. They would collect their goods by donkey at the ports of Galicia. While travelling, they would bring along dried octopus (pulpo) which they would preserve with smoked paprika and rehydrate with olive oil. Today, pulpo has become the showpiece of Galician cuisine and is known all over the world.

The other main ingredient in this dish, cacao, first arrived in Galicia in the 16th century aboard the ships from the New World, after the Spanish had conquered the Aztec Empire. The descendants of the Maragatos were the ones who brought cacao to the town of Astorga in the north and from there to the rest of Spain.

These Maragatos seem to have been very creative and inventive people. Perhaps out of necessity. Inspired by the spirit of their creativity, I like to combine the foods traded by these merchants centuries ago: octopus, smoked paprika, and chocolate.
Octopus is all muscle and these muscles need to relax for the meat to become tender. Traditionally, the Galicians would slam the dead octopus against a rock to tenderize it. A more pleasant and efficient way of doing this is freezing the octopus.
But in most places, octopus is sold frozen or has been frozen at some point before it reaches a store. Double check this with your fishmonger.
Some people claim that throwing a cork in the pan in which you are cooking your octopus also makes it tender.
Another tradition is to dunk the whole octopus three times in boiling water before you cook it to make sure the skin does not come off. There is no scientific evidence to support this tradition, but it is fun to do.
I like to cook the octopus in seawater just as they do in Spain. The total cooking time depends on the weight of the octopus. About 18–20 minutes per kg/2 lbs.

Serves 4

12–16 cups/3–4 liters of (sea)water
1 tsp salt
3 lbs/1.5 kg octopus
smoked paprika and/or spicy paprika
extra virgin olive oil
coarse sea salt or salt flakes

Pulpo a la Gallega - Galician style octopus
Bring a pot of water with a pinch of salt to a boil. Take the octopus by its head and dunk it three times quickly into the boiling water. The fourth time you leave the octopus in the water. Cover the pan and cook for 30 minutes over low to medium-high heat. It is fully cooked when you can pierce one of the thicker parts of the tentacles with a fork or a skewer. Turn off the heat and let the octopus rest in the water for about 10 minutes. Lift the octopus out of the water and let it drain. Save the cooking water. Cut off the tentacles and using scissors, cut into ½ inch slices. Place the slices on a plate or board. Sprinkle with smoked paprika or spicy paprika and drizzle with olive oil. Finish off with coarse salt or salt flakes.

Serving suggestion: Serve with one of the mashes (see recipe on page 158).

Variation: Drizzle with smoked paprika-garlic oil (see recipe on page 168).

Pulpo a la plancha - grilled octopus
Boil the octopus as in the previous recipe. Cut off the tentacles and sauté in 1 tbsp olive oil in a cast-iron pan (or a grill pan) for about 4 minutes over medium high heat. Sprinkle with coarse sea salt or salt flakes. Score the tentacles.

Serving suggestion: Serve with one of the mashes (see recipes below) and aioli (see recipes on page 166) and drizzle with smoked paprika-garlic oil. (see recipe on page 168)

-Puré cremoso de patatas-
1 lb/500 g starchy potatoes
salt
½ cup/100 ml potato water
1 cup/200 ml heavy cream
3 tbsp/60 ml extra virgin olive oil
black pepper

Puré cremoso de patatas - creamy mashed potatoes
Boil the potatoes in salted water for about 20 minutes. Drain the potatoes but save ½ cup of the water. Puree the potatoes with a fork or a masher. Mix the potato water with the cream, olive oil, salt and pepper. Add the mashed potato and mix until smooth. Season with salt and pepper.

-Puré cremoso de patatas y azafrán-
1 lb/500 g starchy potatoes
salt
7–8 saffron threads
½ cup/100 ml potato cooking water
2 tbsp olive oil
1 tbsp crème fraîche or heavy cream
black pepper
2 tbsp/20 g white chocolate

Puré cremoso de patatas y azafrán - creamy saffron mashed potatoes
Boil the potatoes in salted water for about 20 minutes. Drain the potatoes but save ½ cup of the water. Dissolve the saffron in the potato water. Puree the potatoes with a fork or a masher and add the saffron water, olive oil and crème fraîche or cream. The texture can be a little liquid. Season with salt and pepper. Grate some white chocolate on top.

Variation: Substitute the potato cooking water with milk or with the water in which you have cooked the octopus.

-Puré cremoso de patatas violetas-
1 lb/500 g purple potatoes
(Truffe de Chine)
salt
4 tsp olive oil
black pepper
2 tbsp/20 g white chocolate

Puré cremoso de patatas violetas - creamy purple mashed potatoes
Cube the potatoes, boil in salted water for about 10 minutes and drain. Puree with a fork or masher, adding the olive oil. Season with salt and pepper. Grate some white chocolate on top.

-Puré cremoso de coliflor, chocolate blanco y vanilla-
1 head of cauliflower
salt
½ cup/100 ml olive oil
½ cup/100 ml heavy cream
½ vanilla bean
2 tbsp/20 g white chocolate

Puré cremoso de coliflor, chocolate blanco y vanilla - creamy mashed cauliflower with white chocolate and vanilla

Break the cauliflower into florets and boil in salted water for about 10 minutes. Drain and puree with the olive oil, the cream and the seeds scraped from the inside of the vanilla bean. Grate some white chocolate on top.

🍷 A fine white wine with character such as an Albariño.

¡Vieiras a la gallega!
— Galician style Scallops —

Un canto a Galicia, hey, tierra de mi padre. Un canto a Galicia, hey, que es mi tierra madre. Teño morriña, hey... This translates as: "An ode to Galicia, hey, the land of my father. An ode to Galicia, hey, my motherland. I'm homesick, hey."

I haven't quite decided whether I am a fan of Julio Iglesias' music, but I love the way he sings about his nostalgia for Galicia, the 'land' of his parents. My nostalgia for Galicia is related to the wonderful summers I spent there during my teenage years and everything that came with that...

Whenever I have to celebrate something or feel nostalgic about those days, I prepare this dish.

Serves 4

1 onion
1 garlic clove
3.5 oz/100 g Serrano or Iberian ham
2 tbsp olive oil plus extra for drizzling
salt
1 bay leaf
1 tsp smoked paprika
½ cup/100 ml white wine
2 tbsp lemon juice
black pepper
12 scallops
2 tbsp bread crumbs
flat-leaf parsley

Preheat the oven to 390°F/200°C. Dice the onion, garlic and ham. Heat the olive oil in a skillet and sauté the onion over medium-high heat with a pinch of salt for about 8 minutes or until soft. After 4 minutes, add the ham, garlic, bay leaf and smoked paprika. Stir well and make sure the paprika does not burn. Cook for about 10 minutes to caramelize the mixture. Add the wine and the lemon juice and allow to simmer for another 10 minutes over low heat until it has reduced by half. If needed, season with salt and pepper. Remove from heat and set aside.

Divide the scallops over 4 greased oven dishes and cover with the sauce. Sprinkle with bread crumbs. Place the dishes under the broiler for 5–7 minutes until the bread crumbs are golden brown. Garnish with some parsley and serve at once.

Serving suggestion- Serve with creamy saffron mashed potatoes (recipe on page 158)

Variation: You can also prepare the scallops with chorizo.

Serves 4

-Scallops with chorizo-
3.5 oz/100 g chorizo (one piece)
2 tbsp flat-leaf parsley
8 scallops
salt
black pepper
juice of ½ lemon
arugula

Finely slice the chorizo and chop the parsley. Heat the olive oil in a heavy skillet and sauté the chorizo slices for about 1 minute each side over low to medium-high heat. Remove from the pan and set aside. In the same oil, sauté the scallops with a pinch of salt and pepper for about 1½ minutes over medium-high heat. Remove the scallops from the pan and keep warm. Put the chorizo back in the pan with the lemon and the parsley (keep some for serving) and sauté quickly over high heat until the lemon juice has somewhat reduced. If needed, add some olive oil. Serve the scallops with the slices of chorizo leaning against them. Drizzle with the left-over chorizo oil from the pan and garnish with the parsley and arugula.

🍷 A Galician white wine such as an Albariño.

¡Holy aioli!

It all started with MasterChef Holland 2015, the first episode. The assignment was to make a dish where garlic took center stage. There I was, a contestant who had signed up just for fun. Why? Because I like to cook. I wasn't necessarily in it to win.

My Spanish family lives in Ibiza and I love this island. It's my second home. If there is one thing I eat every day when I'm there, it's aioli. Aioli is served in every restaurant or bar. For this reason, it was immediately clear to me what I should prepare to surprise the MasterChef judges. And surprised they were! They started a discussion about the fact that I didn't use salt. They didn't understand me and I didn't understand them; but, during the course of the series, I started taking their advice when it came to salt. It definitely enhances all of the flavors. I grabbed every chance I had during the taping of Masterchef to make the perfect aioli. At home I do the same and aioli is always part of my diet. I often prepare variations, but the basic ingredients are always the same: egg, sunflower oil or olive oil, garlic and salt.

Sunflower oil lends a slightly milder flavor and a different color to aioli compared to olive oil. It is fun to alternate between using the two oils. You can also vary the amount of garlic. Make sure to remove the germ of the garlic to avoid a bitter taste. If you like a softer, sweeter and nuttier flavored aioli, use roasted garlic.

-Roasted garlic-
one whole head of garlic

Ajo asado - roasted garlic
Preheat the oven to 390°F/200°C. Wrap the garlic in tinfoil and roast it in the oven for about 30 minutes. Let it cool. Slice the top of the whole garlic and then squeeze the desired amount of roasted garlic from the cloves.

-Basic aioli-
1 egg, room temperature
salt
1-3 garlic cloves
1 tbsp lemon juice
1 cup/250 ml sunflower oil or olive oil

Aioli básico - Basic Aioli
Put the egg, the pinch of salt, the garlic and the lemon juice in a measuring cup. Place an immersion blender on the bottom of the measuring cup and carefully add the oil. Turn the blender on but do not move it around. When the mixture is emulsified, you can carefully lift the blender up and down until it has reached the desired thickness. Taste and if needed, add salt. If it is too thick, add some water.

Aioli de azafrán - Saffron aioli
Using a mortar and pestle, finely grind a pinch of saffron (5-8 threads) and add to the basic aioli.

Aioli de naranja y miel - Aioli with orange and honey
Add the zest of ½ an orange and 2 tbsp honey to the basic aioli.

Aioli de pimentón - Smoked paprika aioli
Add ½–1 tsp smoked paprika to the basic aioli.

Aioli de tinta de calamar - Squid ink aioli
Add 1–2 packets of squid ink (depending how dark you want it to be) to the basic aioli.

Aioli de ajo negro - Black garlic aioli
Use black garlic rather than regular garlic.

Aioli de ajo ahumado - Smoked garlic aioli
Use smoked garlic instead of regular garlic.

Aioli cremoso - Extra creamy aioli
Add 2 tbsp crème fraîche or 1 tbsp heavy cream to the basic aioli.

Aioli cremoso de cognac - Creamy aioli with Cognac
Add 1 tbsp Cognac and 3 tbsp créme fraiche to the basic aioli.

Aioli de coco - Coconut aioli
Add 2 tbsp of coconut cream or 1 tbsp of coconut milk to the basic aioli.

Aioli de gin tonic - Gin and Tonic aioli
Add 1 tsp Gin and 1 tbsp Tonic to the basic aioli.

Aioli de jamón serrano o ibérico - Aioli with Serrano ham or Iberian ham
Add some crispy Serrano or Iberian ham (see recipe on page 118) to the basic aioli.

Aioli de pera - Pear aioli
Puree ½ ripe pear and add to the basic aioli.

Aioli con pimiento de Sichuan - Aioli with Sichuan pepper
Add ¼ tsp powdered Sichuan pepper to the basic aioli.

¡Aceites aromatizados!
— Flavored olive oils —

Flavored oils are indispensable to me. They are easy to prepare, delicious, colorful and beautiful. You can use them with almost any dish. Drizzle them over tapas, toasted bread, soup, vegetables, meat or fish, rice, and potatoes. You can even fry an egg in a flavored oil.
I store the oils in glass jars or bottles in the refrigerator. After two weeks all the flavors have blended. Use them at room temperature. Before using, shake well and strain through a sieve.
They also make great gifts. Attach an attractive label to a bottle and give it to a friend or a loved one.

-Smoked paprika-garlic oil-
2 garlic cloves
2/3 cup/150 ml extra virgin olive oil
2 tsp smoked paprika

Aceite de ajo y pimentón - Smoked paprika-garlic oil
Slice the garlic as finely as possible. Heat the olive oil in a pan to 140°F/60°C and sauté the garlic over low heat until the oil starts to bubble. Remove from heat and allow to cool. Add the smoked paprika and stir well. Place the pan back on the burner and cook for another 1–2 minutes over low heat until the garlic turns golden brown.

Suggestion: Prepare the oil ahead of time and let it sit in the refrigerator for about 12 hours. The color will intensify to an even deeper red.

-Smoked paprika oil-
200 ml olive oil
4 tsp smoked paprika

Aceite de pimentón - Smoked paprika oil
Heat the olive oil in a pan over low heat to 140°F/60°C. Add the smoked paprika and stir well. Remove from heat and allow to cool.

Suggestion: Strain the oil through a coffee filter or a dish towel to filter out sediment.

-Parsley-garlic oil-
2 cups/50 g flat-leaf parsley, leaves only
2 garlic cloves
1 cup/250 ml extra virgin olive oil

Aceite de ajo y perejil - Parsley-garlic oil
Puree the parsley and the garlic with the olive oil in a blender. If needed, strain through a sieve.

Variation: Substitute the garlic with roasted garlic (recipe on page 166)

-Saffron olive oil-
pinch of saffron (5 threads)
1 rosemary sprig
1 strip of shaved orange skin
1 cup/250 ml extra virgin olive oil

Aceite aromatizado con azafrán, romero y naranja - Flavored oil with saffron, rosemary and orange
Using a mortar and pestle, just lightly crush the saffron. Heat the olive oil with the saffron, rosemary and orange peel over low to medium-high heat for about 10 minutes until it starts to bubble. Remove from heat, cover the pan and allow to cool.

¡Mermelada de chorizo, mango y tónica!
— Chorizo-mango-tonic-jelly —

This might sound like a very strange combination, but I always have a jar of this concoction in my refrigerator. This might be because I always have all three ingredients in stock. This jelly is dream for carnivores and gourmands. I have even managed to convince some vegetarians to try it. The Tonic is a nod to a famous tapa from Master Chef Juan Mari Azak which uses these three ingredients.

jelly jar (1 cup/250 ml)

3,5 oz/100 g chorizo (Spanish dried and cured sausage)
1 tbsp olive oil
1 tbsp/20 g finely chopped red onion
4 oz/125 g cubed mango
2 tbsp/20-25 ml honey
4 dates or 2 tbsp raisins
1 tbsp vinegar
½ cup/125 ml Tonic
salt

Finely chop the chorizo and sauté it in tbsp olive oil for about 1 minute over medium-high heat. Remove the chorizo from the pan and sauté the onion and the mango in the same oil for about 5 minutes. Add the chorizo and the honey and sauté over medium-high heat for another minute until everything has caramelized. Chop the dates or raisins. Add the vinegar, Tonic, dates/raisins and a pinch of salt to the pan. Cook for 30 minutes over low heat until the mixture has thickened. Put it in the glass jelly jar and keep refrigerated.

Serving suggestion: Delicious with Manchego cheese or as a spread on a slice of bread as a base for tapas.

¡Pimientos confitados!
— Pepper jelly —

The Spanish languages is beautiful and extremely seductive. Try having your lover say *pimientos confitados* or *dulce de tomate* and your mouth will water.
Just a teaspoon of this sweet yumminess is delicious combined with something savory.

2 jelly jars (1 cup/250 ml)

1 lb/500 g red bell peppers
½ lb/250 g sugar
½ cup/110 ml vinegar
¼ cup/50 ml water
salt

Deseed and dice the bell peppers. Put the peppers with all the other ingredients in a saucepan and let the mixture simmer for 45 minutes over low heat until the mixture has reduced to a thick jelly. Stir at frequent and regular intervals. Divide over the two jelly jars.

Serving suggestion: Delicious with bread or with pan con tomate (see recipe on page 38) or with meat, fish or cheese.

¡Sal ibérica con toque ahumado!
— Iberian salt with a smoky touch —

Salt enhances all flavors and can also add a touch of elegance to any dish. What's not to like? Salt has always been highly valued, in the old days it was even used as a form of payment. The word "salary" is derived from the Latin word *sal* which means salt.

Chorizo, the typical Spanish sausage is mainstay of Iberian cuisine and is used in many different recipes. An important ingredient in chorizo is the smoked paprika which gives this sausage its special, smoky flavor. In this book, I have made a lot of vegetarian versions of chorizo dishes. In order to stay as close as possible to the original flavor of the chorizo, I have added the chorizo spices and herbs to this salt mixture. If you're vegetarian, or just like to skip meat every now and then, this Iberian salt is a wonderful alternative substitute to give any dish that extra smoky Spanish touch.

Makes about 1.5 oz/40 gr

2 tbsp (coarse) salt
1 tsp smoked paprika
1 tsp dried thyme
1 tsp dried parsley
1 tsp onion powder
½ tsp black pepper
½ tsp garlic powder

Mix all ingredients and keep them in a jar or container with a cover. If using coarse salt, you can keep the mixture in empty salt grinder and grind it as needed.

¡Salsa romesco!
— Romesco sauce —

A real salsa Romesco is made with dried ñora peppers, a special kind of Spanish pepper which has a sweet flavor. In Spain you can buy these everywhere. I once spotted them at a convenience store between the chewing gum and the girlie magazines. Outside of Spain however, there are not readily available. A good alternative is roasted red bell peppers combined with pimentón, Spanish smoked paprika. Pimentón is essentially ground smoked ñora peppers.

There are many versions of this sauce. I like to experiment and vary the amounts of the ingredients and the texture of the sauce. This is what they do in Spain. You can vary the quantity of nuts to make the sauce coarser or finer. You can vary the amount of oil/vinegar to make it more or less liquid. I prefer to make a version which goes easy on the tomatoes (you don't want it to be a tomato sauce) and the texture is quite coarse and nutty. If possible, prepare the sauce a day in advance so the flavors have time to blend.

Serves 4

- 1 red bell pepper
- 2 tomatoes
- 1 garlic head, unpeeled
- 1–2 pieces of white bread (50 g)
- 2 tbsp olive oil
- coarse sea salt
- ½ cup/80 g hazelnuts or ¼ cup/40 g hazelnuts and ¼ cup/40 g almonds
- 3 tbsp/50 ml olive oil
- ½ tbsp Sherry vinegar
- salt
- black pepper
- ½–1 tsp smoked paprika

Preheat the oven to 350°F/180°C. Place the bell pepper, tomatoes, garlic and bread in an oven dish. Drizzle with olive oil and a pinch of coarse sea salt. Bake for about 45 minutes. You can remove the bread earlier once it is crunchy. In the meantime, dry roast the nuts for about 2 minutes in a skillet over low to medium-high heat until golden brown.

Remove the dish from the oven, allow to cool. Peel the pepper and the tomatoes. Cut the top off the garlic and squeeze 2–3 of the roasted cloves into a blender. Add the bread, tomatoes, bell pepper and the nuts. Add the liquid that is left in the oven dish, 3 tbsp olive oil and the Sherry vinegar. Puree and season with salt, pepper and the smoked paprika.

Suggestion: You might be able to buy ñora peppers online or at a Spanish specialty store.

Variation: Add some chili flakes for some extra spice.

¡Torrijas!
— Spanish (French) toast —

When I was a young teenager, while visiting my Spanish family's home it was still customary for the children to eat in the kitchen with the maid. The adults would eat in the dining room at the same time. It was essentially the same meal but with a slightly different consistency. For the children, almost everything was pureed, except for the fries. I didn't like this very much, given that I had perfectly good teeth, had already experienced my first period and knew what it was like to be in love with Spanish boys.
The only thing that made up for having to eat mush was the promise of dessert: *torrijas*, the Spanish version of French toast.

In those days, there were all kinds of stories about torrijas. For instance, eating torrijas was supposed to ease labors pains. This was reassuring to me, not that I was really worried about these as a teenager during those long summers in Spain.
One of the things I used to do to kill time was to visit the chapel across the street from my aunts' house in the late afternoon after eating the torrijas. I was obsessed with the statue of the beautiful Maria and the statue of Jesus on the cross. Going to the chapel was a little scary but at the same time a bit exciting since there was not much else to do.

There is actually some religious symbolism to eating torrijas. They symbolize the resurrection of Jesus. The (old) bread symbolizes Jesus who died on the cross. The dipping of the bread in milk represents the washing and wrapping of the body of Christ. The frying symbolizes Jesus' suffering and the process of bringing Jesus back to life. Traditionally, torrijas are served around Easter but nowadays you can find them on restaurant menus almost year-round. One time I ate torrijas made with brioche. This was so delicious that it was scary, almost as scary as the statue of Jesus on the cross in the chapel near my aunt's house.

These days they try to scare us with something else: sugar. And they're right, so I don't add sugar to the milk in my torrijas recipe even though it goes against tradition. It's definitely worth trying.

Serves 4

-Torrijas-
1 cup/300 ml whole milk
1/3 cup 100 ml heavy cream
1 cinnamon stick
1 small strip of finely shaved lemon skin
1 small strip of finely shaved orange skin
salt
4 soft white rolls (ideally milk rolls)
2 tbsp butter
1 tbsp sugar
Additional (cane) sugar for caramelization

-Custard sauce-
1 egg yolk
1 tbsp sugar
1 tsp cornstarch
1 tbsp milk
the leftover milk/cream mixture in which the rolls have soaked
Optional
1 tbsp almond powder

Mix the milk with the cream in a saucepan and add the cinnamon stick, the orange and lemon zest and a pinch of salt. Slowly bring to a boil and then remove from heat.
Set aside to cool and allow the flavors to blend. (You can prepare this mixture a day in advance and refrigerate overnight). Strain the milk mixture through a sieve. Cut the milk rolls into rectangles. Soak these slices in the milk mixture. Don't soak them too long, you want them to stay in one piece. Remove the roll slices from the milk mixture and drain. Save the leftover milk mixture for the custard sauce.

Prepare the custard sauce

Whisk the egg yolk with the sugar. Dissolve the cornstarch in 1 tbsp milk. Heat the milk cream mixture in which you have soaked the bread rolls and add the cornstarch paste and the whisked egg yolk. Stir well. Cook for 5 minutes over low heat until the sauce has thickened. Keep stirring! If needed, add some almond powder. Cover with plastic wrap and allow to cool.

Heat the butter with the sugar in a skillet. Fry the rolls over medium-high heat for about 5 minutes on each side until they are golden brown all over. Remove from the pan and let them rest until they have firmed up. Sprinkle with (cane) sugar and caramelize with a crème brûlée torch.

Serve with the custard sauce.

Serving suggestion: Delicious with vanilla or mocha ice cream.

Variations:
-substitute the milk rolls with brioche or regular white bread.
-add 1 star anise pod and/or 1 crushed cardamom pod to the milk mixture.
-add a few drops of orange blossom water to the custard sauce to get that Southern-Spanish flavor.
-crumble a few cookies next to the ice cream when serving.
-spread some almond custard on the torrija, sprinkle with the sugar and caramelize with a crème brûlée torch.

A sweet wine such as a Moscatel (unless you are serving the torrijas for breakfast...).

¡Panellets!
— Catalonian All Saints' Day cookies —

All Saints' Day is the festival celebrated on November 1st in honor of all the saints and martyrs of the Roman Catholic Church. There are a lot of saints and martyrs, just as there are a lot of 'high-end' ingredients in these cookies. Traditionally *paneletts* are eaten on this holiday, mainly in Catalonia but also in Ibiza. These cookies are made with almond flour and pine nuts, which are both pricy ingredients but for a special occasion these cookies are definitely worth it.

Makes about 30

½ lb/250 g sweet potatoes
about ½ cup/125 g sugar
salt
grated zest of 1 lemon
2 eggs
3 cups/400 g almond flour
1 ½ cups/250 g pine nuts

Boil the unpeeled sweet potatoes for about 15–20 minutes until cooked. Peel and mash them with a fork while they are still warm. Add the sugar, a pinch of salt and the lemon zest and mix until it is a compact mass and the sugar has dissolved. Beat one egg and add to the mixture. Add the almond flour and mix well. Let the dough rest in the refrigerator for at least 30 minutes or overnight. Preheat the oven to 350°F/180°C. Knead the dough with your hands. Form the dough into 1.5 inch/4cm balls. Roll the balls in the pine nuts and gently press the nuts into the cookies. Beat the yolk of the other egg and brush it over the pine nuts. Arrange the cookies on a baking sheet (covered with baking paper) and bake for 15–20 minutes until golden.

Variation: Substitute the pine nuts with chocolate chips, chopped hazelnuts or shaved coconut.

🍷 Cava.

¡Tarta de Santiago!
— Almond cake from Santiago —

This is a very traditional dessert from Santiago de Compostela and it is named for the apostle Santiago (Saint James), the patron saint of Spain. The cross on this cake is a reference to the sword of Santiago, the symbol of his noble character. Unfortunately, it is also symbolic of the way he died since he was beheaded with a sword. Little is known about the origins of this cake. It is believed to date back to the Middle Ages. Almonds used to be very expensive, therefore this cake was reserved for those with deep pockets. Almonds are still not cheap, but you only need 1 cup for this recipe and the other ingredients will not break the bank.

Serves 10-12

9 oz/250 g of unpeeled almonds
1 ¼ cup/250g sugar
½-1 tsp cinnamon
grated zest of 1 lemon
5 eggs
1 tbsp butter or olive oil
confectioners' sugar

Optional: piece of cardboard to make a stencil for the St. James Cross decoration (look for this on the internet)

Preheat the oven to 350°F/180°C. Using an almond grinder or food processor, grind half the almonds as finely as possible and chop the other half coarsely so they still retain some texture. Mix all of the almonds with the sugar, cinnamon and lemon zest. Add the eggs one by one and mix with a spatula. Do not beat the mixture. Only add the following egg once the previous one has been absorbed into the batter. Line the bottom of a 9-inch springform pan with parchment paper, grease the sides and pour in the batter. (You can grease the parchment paper as well to make sure the cake does not stick). Bake the cake for 20 minutes until it is golden brown. While the cake is in the oven you can cut out the shape of the St James Cross. Remove the cake from the oven and let it cool for 10 minutes. Remove the outer ring of the springform pan, place the St. James cross stencil on the cake and use a sieve to dust the confectioners' sugar over the top. Remove the stencil to reveal the shape of the cross on the cake.

Preparation suggestion: Insert a toothpick into the center of the cake, when it comes out clean, it is done.

Variations:
- The original recipe calls for 1 ¼ cup of sugar, but I like to make it with ½ cup or even 1/3 cup. It tastes just as good. Note: when using less sugar also cut out one of the eggs.
- You can use store bought almond meal instead of the finely ground almonds.
- First beat the eggs with the sugar into a creamy foam, then add the rest of the ingredients. Gently mix it all together while allowing plenty of air to enter into the batter.
- Add a little Pedro Ximénez, Port wine, Cognac or dessert wine in the batter for extra flavor.

🍷 A sweet wine such as Pedro Ximénez, Port wine, Cognac or dessert wine.

¡Arroz con leche asturiano cremoso!
— Creamy rice pudding from Asturias —

I like to add my own twist to recipes. I have a curious nature, a creative spirit and I am a little bit of a know-it-all. But in honor of my grandmother, I barely altered this recipe, except for the sugar.

Serves 4

2/3 cup/150 g short-grain rice
1 cup/250 ml water
salt
4 cups/1 l whole milk
just under ½ cup/100 ml heavy cream
1 cinnamon stick
2 strips of finely shaved lemon skin
¼–½ cup/ 50–100 g sugar, to taste
3 tbsp/30 g butter
1 tsp anise liqueur

Boil the rice in the water with a pinch of salt over low heat for about 5 minutes, then drain. Pre-boiling the rice will 'open up' the grains in order to absorb all the flavors later on. Combine the milk, cream, cinnamon, lemon skin and rice and bring to a boil. Cook for about 50 minutes over low heat until the rice is tender and creamy. Stir regularly. Mix in the butter and sugar and cook for another 10 minutes over low heat, stirring occasionally. Add a pinch of salt and the anise liqueur. Let it cool but stir occasionally to prevent a film from forming on top.

Serving suggestion: Add a dash of cinnamon on top and some shaved almonds

🍷 Something sweet such as a Port wine or a sweet Sherry.

¡Mantecadas de Astorga!
— Mini butter cakes from Astorga —

A *mantecada* is a small pound cake with a rich history. It was created by a nun in a convent in the town of Astorga halfway through the 19th century. *Manteca* means butter in Spanish and, as the name suggests, it's what gives these cakes their rich, buttery flavor and velvety texture. In Spain they come in a square or rectangular shape and are wrapped in paper. For this recipe, I often use a muffin tin so they will come out round. Just like some Spanish wines and olive oils, mantecadas have a DO (Denominación de Origen) label meaning they have a protected status.

As a little girl I was intrigued by the fresh milk that was delivered to my grandmother's house every morning. Fresh milk, straight from the cow, still warm delivered in a metal container at the service entrance to her house. I was told the milk was creamy and sweet and full of flavor, but I never wanted to drink it.
The cream that would form on top after a day was another story. I used to watch my grandmother skimming the cream from the top of the milk can with a big ladle. She would spoon the cream into a glass jar and let it sit for a while. When it had the right consistency, she would use it for baking cake. That was definitely worth the wait.
Astorga itself also has a rich history and many attractions. It is a small city along the Camino de Santiago pilgrimage route. The sale of mantecadas is a huge source of income for the town. Astorga is near Ponferrada, my grandmother's hometown. Whenever I'm in the neighborhood, I stop to buy some of these calorie bombs. They remind me of my grandmother's cake.

Makes 24

2 sticks/250 g butter
1 ¼ cup/250 g sugar
salt
6 eggs, at room temperature
2 cups/250 g all-purpose flour

Optional:
Cinnamon

Preheat the oven to 350°F/180 °C. Melt the butter in a saucepan over low heat. Pour the melted butter in a bowl. Add the sugar and a pinch of salt and beat with an electric mixer. Add the eggs one by one and keep mixing. Place the flour (and some cinnamon) in a sifter or a sieve and sift bit by bit into the mixture. Beat until smooth.
Line a muffin pan with paper baking cups. Spoon the batter into the cups until they are half full. Bake for about 10 minutes until the cakes turn a golden color.

🍷 A Muscatel or a Sherry.

¡Pan con chocolate, aceite de oliva y sal!
— Bread with chocolate, olive oil and salt —

I must have been around 8 years old. A long time ago. I have vague memories of wonderful long summers in Spain. To bring back these memories, I have to make do with black and white photographs. But sometimes I dream of these summers.

It's always the same dream, in black and white. The colors of the *merienda*, or afternoon snack we used to get when we were kids. In this case a crunchy piece of baguette with a chunk of chocolate inside. We were told it was good for us, it would make us grow tall. There was nothing decadent about it.

I have transformed this simple snack into a decadent dessert, with the same contrast of the white bread and the creamy chocolate. There is nothing healthy about it, but it is so delicious that it makes me happy. I am convinced you live longer when you're happy.

Serves 4

2–3 sprigs of rosemary
¼ cup/65 ml heavy cream
3.5 oz/100 g dark chocolate
2 tsp brown sugar
1 tbsp/10 g butter
1/2 baguette
extra virgin olive oil
coarse sea salt or salt flakes

Pour the cream into a saucepan and add 1 sprig of rosemary. In another pan, heat the chocolate au bain-marie (or in a double boiler) until it melts. Bring the cream to a boil over low heat and remove the rosemary. Once it boils, pour the cream into the chocolate in two batches while stirring. Add the sugar and butter and stir well. Pour the mixture into a bowl, place the remaining rosemary sprigs on top and cover. Place in the fridge.

Preheat the oven to 350°F/180°C. Slice the baguette into very thin slices and divide these over a baking pan lined with parchment paper. Drizzle with olive oil. Place the pan under the broiler for about 5 minutes until the bread is crunchy and golden brown. Drizzle 1–2 tbsp olive oil on a dessert plate. Using two spoons, shape the chocolate into 'quenelles', egg shaped dollops and place these in the olive oil.

Sprinkle some salt flakes on the quenelles. Place one slice of toasted bread in each chocolate quenelle and finish off with a bit of rosemary.

Suggestion: Make a few extra toasted baguette slices. You can save them for a few days and they are very good with a bit of Manchego cheese or with a dipping sauce.

🍷 A red wine with character such as Mencia.

¡Churros con chocolate con chispa!
— Churros with a spicy chocolate sauce —

When the Spanish conquered Mexico in 1521 they discovered all the wonderful things you can do with cacao beans. Apart from all the sweet temptations, you can also use chocolate in savory dishes such as in Salvador Dali's favorite dish: lobster in chocolate sauce.
Churros are actually also a savory treat. According to the traditional recipe, there is no sugar in the batter. The savory churro is delicious in combination with the chocolate. You can sprinkle some sugar on the churros just before eating if you like them a little sweet.

The origin of churros is a mystery. Some claim they have Chinese roots, just like me.
In spite of my roots, I have never been to China, but I have spent a lot of time in the mountains in Spain, so I think I'll go with the theory that churros were invented by Spanish shepherds. According this theory, the name comes from *churra*, a specific breed of sheep. Churros have a shape similar to the horns of these sheep. Supposedly, the shepherds who lived with these sheep in the mountains invented churros, since they were easy to cook over an open fire and required very few ingredients.
The beauty of the traditional churro is the simplicity of the ingredients. The golden rule is one cup of flour to one cup of salted water.

Makes 10

-Chocolate sauce-
2 cups/500 ml whole milk
1 tbsp cornstarch
1 cup/175 g dark chocolate
½ tsp cinnamon

Optional
pinch of black pepper
or Sichuan pepper

-Dough-
1 cup water
1 tsp salt
1 cup all-purpose flour
olive oil
sugar

Heat the milk over low heat. Dissolve the cornstarch in 1 tbsp cold milk. Chop the chocolate and add to the milk. Once the chocolate has melted, add in the cornstarch paste until the sauce has thickened. Add the cinnamon and if you like a kick, add some pepper as well.

There is a special trick to preparing the sponge-like dough for the real traditional Spanish churros. After you have measured the flour, you scoop out one level tablespoon and set it aside to be used later. Place the flour (minus the one tbsp) in a large bowl. Boil the water with the salt and pour it into the flour bowl. Stir the dough with a wooden spatula for about 1 minute until soft peaks form. The dough should not be too liquid otherwise it will absorb too much oil. Add the tbsp flour which you had set aside. Test the dough by pressing it with the palm of your hand. Your palm should stay clean.

Cover the dough and let it rest for 5-10 minutes. Transfer the dough to a piping bag with a star tip. Heat the olive oil in a heavy pan to about 350°F/180°C. Use just enough oil so the churros are covered. Test the temperature of the oil by tossing in a bit of dough and if it starts to 'dance', the oil it hot enough. Carefully pipe a line of dough into the hot oil and cut with scissors. Only fry about 1 or 2 churros at a time. Fry for 2-3 minutes until golden brown. Drain on a paper towel. If you like them sweet, drizzle with sugar. Serve at once and dip into the warm chocolate sauce.

🍷 A sweet wine or liqueur, such as a Moscatel or Hierbas de Ibiza.

¡Greixonera con café Caleta!
— Ibizan bread pudding with Caleta coffee —

Ensaimadas are sweet, spiral-shaped breads from the Balearic Islands. They come in pretty, round or hexagonal boxes but you don't want to be seen carrying these around the Ibiza airport. The name ensaimada comes from the Arabic word *saim* which means lard, which is often used in Spanish breads and pastries. The traditional Ibizan *greixonera* desert is prepared with the leftover ensaimadas from the day before. The day-old bread actually absorbs the milk better.

Greixonera is the name of the clay bowl used to prepare the desert. It is a bread pudding served with a caramel sauce. It's a little too sweet for my taste, so I like to serve it with fruit instead. Since ensaimadas are only available on the Balearic Islands, I use croissants for this recipe. I use less sugar than the original recipe (1 cup) since there is already enough sugar in the croissants.

Serves 4-8

-Bread Pudding-
2 cups/500 ml whole milk
½ cinnamon stick
1 small strip of finely shaved lemon skin
butter
2 croissants
3 eggs
1/4 cup/50 g sugar

-Optional-
1–2 tbps anise liqueur

-Café Caleta-
4 tbps sugar
1 strip of finely shaved lemon skin
1 strip of finely shaved orange skin
1 cinnamon stick
1 cup/250 ml Spanish Brandy
2 cups/500 ml coffee

Heat the milk with the cinnamon and the strip of lemon skin and bring to a boil. Remove the pan from the heat and let it cool off. Remove the cinnamon stick and the lemon skin. Preheat the oven to 350 °F/180°C. Grease a baking dish with butter.
Rip the croissants into pieces. Whisk the eggs and mix in the sugar. Add the milk to the eggs and mix well. Add the pieces of croissant. (Add the anise liqueur) Pour the mixture in a baking dish and place in the oven for about 45 minutes. The greixonera is done when you insert a toothpick into the center of the cake and it comes out clean.

Variations:
-Substitute the strip of lemon skin with grated lemon zest
-Use cupcake pan or other baking molds to make individual greixoneras.

Place the sugar, the strips of lemon and orange skin, the cinnamon and the Brandy in a pan. Heat but do not bring to a boil. Using a ladle, scoop the Brandy mixture from the pan and flambé in the ladle.

A Spanish liqueur such as Licor 43, Hierbas de Ibiza or a Spanish Brandy.

¡Crema catalana al azafrán!
— Saffron crema catalana —

This *crema catalana* proves that saffron is not only delicious in savory dishes but also in desserts. I have added some orange as well to make it even more Spanish.
The saffron adds a unique sweet flavor and a special touch to this typical Catalonian dessert. I have used less sugar in this recipe than in a traditional crema catalana.

Serves 4

1 cinnamon stick
1 star-anise pod
2 strips of finely shaved orange skin
1 ½ cups/350 ml whole milk
½ cup/100 ml heavy cream
6 saffron threads or a tiny pinch of saffron powder
4 egg yolks
1/4 cup/50 g sugar
4 tsp/10 g cornstarch
brown sugar

Put the cinnamon stick, star-anise, the strips of orange skin, milk and cream in a saucepan and gently bring to a boil over low heat. Remove from the heat. When using saffron threads, wrap them in tin foil and heat in a pan for about 30 seconds over medium-high heat to release the flavors. Add the saffron threads or saffron powder to the milk and the cream mixture. Allow to infuse for 15 minutes. Whisk the egg yolks, the sugar and the corn starch until light and creamy. If needed, reheat the milk/cream mixture, strain through a sieve and add it to the egg mixture. Bring this combined mixture gently to a boil and cook for 10 minutes while stirring until it has thickened. Divide over 4 ramekins and, allow to cool and then place them in the refrigerator to set for about 2 hours. Sprinkle a thin layer of brown sugar on top of each *crema* and caramelize with a crème brûlée torch. Keep moving the flame to prevent the sugar from burning. Serve at once. If you don't have a torch, turn on your broiler and place the ramekins under the broiler until the sugar has melted and has turned golden brown and crispy.

🍷 A sweet wine or liqueur such as a Moscatel, or Hierbas de Ibiza.

¡Flaó d'Eivissa!
— Ibizan cheesecake —

Traditionally *flaó* was only prepared on Easter Sunday but these days it's available in Ibiza all year round. Flaó is a cake filled with cheese or crème fraiche and *Eivissa* is the local name for Ibiza. This typical Ibizan cheese cake is subtly flavored with mint and aniseed.
Flaó should really be prepared with fresh goat cheese but since most men I know don't like the taste of goat cheese, I love to make flaó with ricotta and mascarpone.

Serves 8–12

-Crust-
2 cups/250 all-purpose flour
1/8 cup/25 g sugar
½ tsp salt
1 tsp aniseed
2 ½ tbsp/30 g butter
2 tbsp extra virgin olive oil
1 egg
2 tbsp anise liqueur
grated zest of ½ lemon

-Filling-
4 eggs
2 ¼ cup/250 g sugar
2/3 cup/150 g mascarpone
1 1/3/350 g ricotta
½ tsp cinnamon
2 tbsp chopped fresh mint with a few leaves left whole

Mix the flour, the sugar, the salt and the aniseed. Stir in the butter and the other ingredients. Knead the dough until it comes together. Wrap the dough in plastic foil and place it in the refrigerator for about 30 minutes.

Beat the eggs and the sugar into a frothy mix. Mix the mascarpone, the ricotta and the cinnamon and stir this into the eggs. Add the chopped mint. Preheat the oven to 330°F/165°C. Remove the dough from the refrigerator and roll it out. Grease a 10-inch pie dish and line with the dough. Add the filling and spread it out to fill the crust. Place in the oven and bake for 45 minutes until done. Allow to cool. Garnish with some fresh mint leaves. Serve cold.

🍷 A sweet wine such as a Moscatel, a sweet Sherry or Hierbas de Ibiza.

¡Rosquillas de anis!
— Aniseed cookies —

Maybe it was the long summer days, the late dinners and the late bedtime, but as a kid I was always sick for a day or two during our summer vacations in Spain.
The symptoms were always those of a mild flu and the best medicine was always *rosquillas*, my grandmother's Easter cookies.
Anise or green anise is an herb that grows throughout Spain and is often used in baked goods and liqueurs. Aniseed is delicious but it also soothes the stomach. In addition, it contains anethole which is beneficial for your respiratory system. I never minded when I didn't feel well during those vacations.

Makes 15

1 egg
¾ cup/75 g sugar
2 tsp/8 g baking powder
grated zest of half a lemon
½ cup/125 ml olive oil
¼ cup/60 ml anise liqueur
2 1/3 cup/300 g all-purpose flour
½–1 tsp anise seed
salt

Preheat the oven to 350°F/180°C. Whisk the egg with the sugar, baking powder and lemon zest. Pour in the olive oil and the liqueur. Add the flour, aniseed and a pinch of salt. Knead the dough until it is firm but elastic. Let the dough rest in the refrigerator for 15 minutes. Shape the dough into 15 equal size balls and then roll these into a sausage shape about 5 inches long. Stick both ends together to make each cookie into a doughnut shape. Place the cookies on a baking tray lined with parchment paper and bake for about 15–20 minutes until done.

🍷 A young sweet wine such as a Moscatel or a sweet Sherry.

¡Sangria de cava estilo Ibiza!
— Ibiza style white sangria with Cava —

Do you want to liven things up and get the party going? Make some sangria with Cava (Spanish Champagne). It will be a guaranteed success.

There are a lot of versions of this decadent drink. I have developed a version for beginners and one for 'the advanced'. The latter version is inspired by the *Sangria de Cava* which they serve at my favorite beach in Ibiza. Whenever I ask for the recipe, they give vague answers, preserving the mystery. All that they'll tell me is: "it has some liqueurs, strawberries, raspberries, banana..." Over the years I've tasted this sangria many times and gathered enough information from the waiters that I think my version comes pretty close.

Serves 8
-White sangria with Vodka-

1 lemon or lime
1 peach/mango/apple/pineapple or other fruit
¼ cup/60 ml Vodka
10 ice cubes
1 bottle Cava Brut

Optional:
2 tbsp sugar

Sangría de cava para avanzados - White sangria for 'the advanced'
Wash the apple, orange and peach and slice thinly. Halve the strawberries and the grapes. Put all the fruit in a large glass pitcher. Pour in the Brandy and the Cointreau. Stir gently and place the pitcher in the refrigerator for 2 hours to allow all the flavors to blend.
Add the ice cubes and the orange juice and stir gently with a wooden spoon. Carefully pour in the Cava while tilting the pitcher to avoid foaming.

Variations:
-in Ibiza they often fill your glass halfway with Cava and then add the Sangria.
-substitute the Brandy with Vodka, Gin or Licor 43.
-add 1–2 tbsp sugar to the fruit mixture and stir carefully.
-substitute the strawberries and grapes with a handful pureed raspberries and half a mashed banana.

Serves 8

-White Sangria for 'the advanced'-
1 apple
1 orange
1 peach
1 small bunch of grapes
4 strawberries
¼ cup/50 ml Spanish Brandy
¼ cup/50 ml Cointreau
10 ice cubes
½ cup/100 ml orange juice
1 bottle Cava Brut

Sangría de cava con vodka para principiantes - Cava Sangria with Vodka for beginners
Slice or cube the fruit and put it in a glass pitcher. Add the Vodka and the sugar (optional).
Place the pitcher in the refrigerator for 2 hours to allow all the flavors to blend. Add the ice cubes and stir gently with a wooden spoon. Carefully pour in the Cava while tilting the pitcher to avoid foaming.

¡Gin tonic español!
— Spanish Gin and Tonic —

Gin and Tonics have made a comeback as a hip cocktail in bars from Amsterdam to New York and everywhere in between. In Spain however, 'gin tonics' as they are called, were already very popular in the eighties. They were everywhere, from the student pub on the campus of Madrid University to the smallest bars in remote mountain villages. I tasted many in my student days in Madrid. At that time there where three main Gin brands: Beefeater, Gordons and Larios, a Spanish brand. Beefeater was a bit more expensive and tasted a lot better. The Spanish versions were cheap and the hangover the next day was included in the price.

Gin and Tonics were served in a long drink glass packed with ice and a slice of lemon which was first run around the rim of the glass. The Gin was never measured but poured from a plastic dispenser attached to the bottle which meant that you wound up with a very generous amount in your glass. On average, the amount of Gin was about twice as much as you would get in a bar in the Netherlands. The Tonic they served was usually Schweppes which is strongly carbonated.

These days you'll still find those same three Gin brands in your average Spanish bar but you'll also see Tanqueray and Bombay Sapphire. In the big clubs and more modern bars you will find a wide selection of Gins as well as Tonics. The Spanish now produce some very nice gins of their own. The best-known Spanish Gin internationally is Gin Mare, which has even won some awards. It's my personal favorite. A clear Gin with an aromatic finish redolent of rosemary, thyme and basil. Nordés is another aromatic Gin from Galicia, distilled from the Albariño grape and fifteen botanical herbs. Both Gins will give this delicious Gin and Tonic with orange, rosemary and chili pepper a wonderful Spanish touch. My husband Daniel makes this Gin and Tonic just the way I like it, with some Spanish fire!

2 sprigs rosemary
ice cubes
¼ cup/60 ml Gin (preferably Spanish, Gin Mare or Nordés)
1 orange wedge
1 orange peel
1 tiny bit of fresh chili pepper (or three pink peppercorns)
tonic (preferable 1724 or some other mild, not overly sweet Tonic)

Optional:
1 additional orange wedge for decoration

Take a large Gin and Tonic glass and a sprig of rosemary. Light the end of the sprig with a match until it starts to smoke. Place the smoking rosemary in the glass and cover so the smoke gets trapped inside. Remove the burnt rosemary sprig from the glass and replace it with a fresh one. Add a lot of ice cubes and pour in the gin. Squeeze the juice from the orange wedge into the glass and drop the wedge in the glass. Rub the rim of the glass with the orange peel and add this to the glass as well. Add a bit of chili pepper or the peppercorns. Pour in as much Tonic as you like. Not too much and preferably pour the Tonic along a bar spoon to keep the fizz. Stir briefly to blend all the flavors. Place an orange wedge on the rim of the glass for decoration. *Salud!* (Cheers!).

¡Vinos españoles!
— Spanish wines

My husband Daniel is half Spanish just as I am and also loves the good life. For both of us, a glass of good wine is very much a part of this. Daniel is an aficionado and a connoisseur of Spanish wines. My personal sommelier.

"Together with France and Italy, Spain is one of the world's top three wine exporting countries. Spain has many wine regions which produce wonderful wines. Rioja is the most well-known region, especially for its deep red *reservas* (reserve wines) with their characteristically robust aftertaste. However, Ribera del Duero is catching up with Rioja in terms of the most popular wines. Both of these red wines are made predominantly with the typical Spanish grape, the Tempranillo, but there are some major differences. The Rioja region is a bit further north, which means the vineyards get more rain than the ones in Ribera del Duero. This latter region is just north of Madrid and is not only drier but also prone to temperature fluctuations. The Rioja region produces twice the volume of wine as Ribera del Duero and offers a greater variety of lighter wines. The Ribera del Duero wines tend have a darker color, even the younger ones. The aftertaste of the Ribera del Duero wines is more reminiscent of dark fruit whereas Riojas have more of a red fruit finish.

Wine is an important element of a Spanish meal and wine preferences tend to be very personal. Therefore, the wines suggestions in this book are my personal preferences.

I find the wines from the North of Spain more interesting than those from the South. I miss a bit of character in the southern wines and they are often a little too sweet for my palate. The South does produce the world-renowned Sherry which can be very dry, but there are also sweet varieties. Pedro Ximénez is Sandra's favorite, not just for drinking but also for cooking.

Through the use of modern technologies and the blending of different grape varieties there are new developments all over Spain which are producing surprising wines. The results of these developments are positive: beautifully balanced wines that score high on renowned wine connoisseur Robert Parker's list. Unfortunately, not all new Spanish wines are available outside the country, such as the Prieto Picudo from León which I highly recommend if you ever find yourself there. This red wine is usually served cold, as is often customary with red wines in Spain (about 14°C /58°F).

For Spanish red wines, my order of preference is: Ribera del Duero, Rioja, Priorat and Toro. I also find certain wines from the from the following regions interesting: Bierzo (northern Spain) Somontano (Aragon, Pyrenees) and Terra Alta (southern Catalonia). Many smaller vineyards offer surprisingly fine wines, but unfortunately these are not readily available outside of Spain. These wines are special because they use grape varieties such as Mencia (from Bierzo) and blends with Cabernet Sauvignon, Monastrel, Merlot and Syrah, as is done in several Catalonian regions. (e.g. Costers de Segre, Terra Alta and Priorat). I don't gravitate to wines from La Mancha or Levante since I don't find them nearly as refined as some other, newer wine varieties from these regions.

When it comes to Spanish white wines, I usually opt for an Albariño or a Rueda but certain white wines from Penedès, Rioja, Castile or Catalonia can also be very interesting. Albariño is obviously produced from the Albariño grape and is known for its minerality because of its coastal location in Galicia in northwestern Spain. Rueda is fruitier and can also be more acidic (it is usually made from Verdejo or Sauvignon Blanc grapes). The crispness of these wines is especially well suited to Spanish fish dishes, which are rich in flavor and even more so under a strong Spanish sun. The older grape vines have smaller grapes with an even richer flavor. Sometimes this is mentioned on the label, for instance with the Centenario.

I also enjoy the Catalonian white wines. Some of them have been aged in oak barrels, which gives them an amber color and a full-bodied flavor. To change it up I like to try different blends such as Chardonnay and Xarel-lo.

I am not a big fan of *rosados*, Spanish rosés. I usually find them too heavy or too sweet. I used to drink *rosado* as a *vino de mesa* (table wine; this is called *clarete* in León), and every now and then I still drink a light *rosado* from Rioja, Catalonia or Ibiza. In general, I am not a big rosé drinker, I'd rather have a French Vin Gris.

Cava (Spanish sparkling wine) predominantly comes from Penedès but is also produced in other areas from the northeast to the southeast of Spain. The varieties are comparable to other sparkling wines; from sweet to *brut nature*, the driest variety. Cava is usually more affordable than the French Cremant, but often just as enjoyable. Other sparkling wines such as Prosecco and Sekt usually are of a lesser quality unless you are willing to spend a pretty penny.

If Spanish wines are not readily available in your area, below are a few suggestions for substitutions. Full-bodied Spanish red wines such as Rioja, Ribera del Duero, Toro and Priorat can be substituted with a Cabernet or blended wines from the Napa Valley (USA). As for white wines, Albariño can be substituted with a crisp Sauvignon Blanc and Rueda wines, which often have a fruity flavor, can be substituted with a fruity Chardonnay."

Daniel Alvarez van der Feltz

Tapas and pinchos

Pincho de champiñones – Mushroom pinchos 18
Pincho de dátil relleno y jamón serrano – Stuffed dates and Serrano ham pinchos 18
Pincho con plátano y jamón serrano – Banana and Serrano ham pinchos 18
Higos asados con jamón ibérico y queso de cabra – Grilled figs with Iberian ham and goat cheese 18
Bomba de la Barceloneta – Potato-meatball Barceloneta style 20
Pan de tinta de calamar – Bread with squid ink 22
Tapa con pan de tinta de calamar – Tapa with squid ink bread 22
Buñuelos de bacalao – Salted cod fritters 24
Croquetas cremosas españolas – Creamy Spanish croquettes 26
Croquetas de jamón ibérico o serrano – Iberian or Serrano ham croquettes 26
Croquetas de gambas – Shrimp croquettes 28
Croquetas vegetarianas – Vegetarian croquettes 28
Tapa de endivias con cabrales y nueces – Endive tapa with Cabrales cheese and walnuts 30
Queso Manchego en aceite de oliva – Manchego cheese marinated in olive oil 32
Chips de berenjenas con miel – Eggplant chips with honey 34
Pan con tomate – Catalan tomato bread 38
Pan con tomate con manchego – Pan con tomate with Manchego cheese 38
Pan con tomate con jamón serrano o ibérico – Pan con tomate with Serrano or Iberian ham 38
Pan con tomate vegetal – Vegetarian pan con tomate 38
Tabla de delicias ibéricas – Spanish Cheese and Charcuterie platter 42
Aceitunas aliñadas con limón, ajo y hinojo – marinated olives with lemon, garlic and fennel 44
Sobrasada vegana – vegan spread (chorizo flavor) 44
Tostada con sobrasada vegana, miel y almendras – Toasted bread with vegan sobrasada, honey and almonds 44
Dulce de tomate – Tomato jam 45
Paté de almendras y aceitunas – Almond-olive spread 45
Mahonesa de moras – Blackberry mayonnaise 45
Crema de aceitunas – Olive spread 45

Soups

Ajoblanco – Almond gazpacho 48
Sopa de pescado vasca – Basque fish soup 50
Fabada vegetal – Vegetarian bean stew 52
Gazpacho cremoso y sedoso – Creamy, silky gazpacho 54
Sopa de lentejas vegetariana – Vegetarian lentil soup 56
Sopa de ajo – Garlic soup 58

Classics

Tortilla de patatas – Spanish omelet 63
Huevos estrellados – Scrumptious fried eggs 66
Patatas bravas – Fried potato cubes with a spicy sauce 68
Pimientos de Padrón – Fried Padron peppers 70
Ensaladilla rusa vegetal – Vegetarian Russian potato salad 72
Coca de escalivada – Ibiza-style pizza with grilled vegetables 74
Migas con uvas y secreto ibérico – Chorizo croutons with grapes and Iberian pork secreto 76
Pan payès fácil ibicenco – Easy peasant bread from Ibiza 78
Paella valenciana – Paella from Valencia 81
Chorizos ibéricos a la sidra con col verde – Cabbage rolls with Iberian sausage 84
Albóndigas con salsa sedosa – Spanish meatballs with a silky tomato-saffron sauce 86
Cordero asado estilo Segovia – Roast leg of lamb Segovian style 88
Rabo de buey con salsa de vino y chocolate – Braised Oxtail in a red wine-chocolate sauce 90
Flamenquines de pollo – Breaded chicken rolls with saffron mayonnaise 92
Empanada gallega de atún – Tuna empanada from Galicia 95
Gambas a la plancha – Grilled shrimp 98
Zarzuela – Spanish fish stew 100
Lubina a la sal aromatizada – Seabass baked in herbed salt crust 102
Gambas al ajillo – Garlic shrimp 104
Mejillones con salsa brava – Mussels in salsa brava 106
Mejillones in escabeche – Marinated mussels 106
Mejillones con salsa de azafrán – mussels with a saffron cream sauce 106
Chipirones rellenos en su tinta – Stuffed squid in ink sauce 109

Healthy

Ensalada de naranja sanguina invernal – Winter salad with blood orange 114
Sandía a la plancha con ensalada de tomate – Grilled watermelon with tomato salad 116
Ensalada ibérica con melón caramelizado – Iberian salad with caramelized melon 118
Ensalada de salpicón de mariscos – Seafood salad 120
Espárragos verdes a la plancha – Grilled asparagus 122
Ensalada escalivada – Roasted vegetable salad 124

Salsa de pimientos asados con nata – Roasted bell pepper cream sauce 124
Ensalada de habas mixtas – Smoky bean salad 128
Puerros caramelizados con salsa romesco – Caramelized leeks with romesco sauce 130
Garbanzos crujientes con espinacas – Crunchy chickpeas with spinach 132
Morcilla vegetariana – Vegetarian blood sausage 134
Paella vegetal – Vegetarian paella 136

Happy Chic
Bocadillo de tinta de calamares – Squid ink bun with calamari 140
Bikini ibérico – Iberian grilled sandwich 142
Tortitas de guisantes – Green Pea pancakes 144
Cupcakes ibéricos – Iberian cupcakes 148
Bacalao con alioli gratinado – Cod with aioli au gratin 151
Bacalao confitado – Cod Confit 152
Arroz negro – Black rice 154
Pulpo a la gallega – Galician style octopus 156
Pulpo a la plancha – Grilled octopus 158
Puré cremoso de patatas – creamy mashed potatoes 158
Puré cremoso de patatas y azafrán – creamy saffron mashed potatoes 158
Puré cremoso de patatas violetas – creamy purple mashed potatoes 158
Puré cremoso de coliflor, chocolate blanco y vanilla – Creamy mashed cauliflower with white chocolate and vanilla 158
Vieiras a la gallega – Galician style scallops 160
Vieiras con chorizo – Scallops with chorizo 160

Holy aioli
Ajo asado – Roasted garlic 166
Alioli básico – Basic Aioli1 66
Alioli de azafrán – Saffron Aioli 166
Alioli de naranja y miel – Aioli with orange and honey 166
Alioli de pimentón – Smoked paprika aioli 166
Alioli de tinta de calamar – Squid ink aioli 166
Alioli de ajo negro – Black garlic aioli 166
Alioli de ajo ahumado – Smoked garlic aioli 166
Alioli cremoso – Extra creamy aioli 166
Alioli cremoso de cognac – Creamy aioli with Cognac 166
Alioli de coco – Coconut aioli 166
Alioli de gin tonic – Gin and Tonic aioli 166
Alioli de jamón serrano o ibérico – Aioli with Serrano or Iberian ham 166
Alioli de pera – Pear aioli 166
Alioli con pimienta de Sichuan – Aioli with Sichuan pepper 166
Aceites aromatizados – Flavored olive oils 168
Aceite de ajo y pimentón – Smoked paprika-garlic oil 168
Aceite de pimentón – Smoked paprika oil 168
Aceite de ajo y perejil – Parsley garlic oil 168
Aceite aromatizado con azafrán, romero y naranja – Flavored oil with saffron, rosemary and orange 168
Mermelada de chorizo, mango y tónica – Chorizo-mango-tonic-jelly 170
Pimientos confitados – Pepper jelly 172
Sal ibérica con toque ahumado – Iberian salt with a smoky touch 174
Salsa romesco – Romesco sauce 176

Sweets
Torrijas – Spanish (French) toast 181
Panellets – Catalonian All Saints' Day cookies 184
Tarta de Santiago – Almond cake from Santiago 186
Arroz con leche asturiano cremoso – Creamy rice pudding from Asturias 188
Mantecadas de Astorga – Mini butter cakes from Astorga 190
Pan con chocolate, aceite de oliva y sal – Bread with chocolate, olive oil and salt 192
Churros con chocolate con chispa – Churros with a spicy chocolate sauce 194
Greixonera con café Caleta – Ibizan bread pudding with Caleta coffee 198
Crema catalana al azafrán – Saffron crema catalana 200
Flaó d'Eivissa – Ibizan cheesecake 202
Rosquillas de anis – Aniseed cookies 204

Cheers
Sangria de cava para avanzados – White sangria for 'the advanced' 208
Sangria de cava con vodka para principiantes – Cava Sangria with Vodka for beginners 208
Gin tonic español – Spanish Gin and Tonic 210
Vinos españoles – Spanish wines 212

Index

Aioli, sauces and oils
Basic Aioli and 13 variations 166
Chorizo-mango-tonic-jelly 170
Flavored olive oils 168
Iberian salt with a smoky touch 174
Pepper jelly 172
Roasted bell pepper cream sauce 124
Romesco sauce 176
Tomato jam 45

Almonds
Almond cake from Santiago 186
Almond gazpacho 48
Almond-olive spread 45
Catalonian All Saints' Day cookies 184
Toasted bread with vegan Sobrasada, honey and almonds 44

Bananas
Banana and Serrano ham pinchos 18
Vegetarian lentil soup with fried plantain garnish 56

Beans
Smoky bean salad 128
Vegetarian bean stew 52
Vegetarian blood sausage 134

Bread
Bread with chocolate, olive oil and salt 192
Iberian grilled sandwich 142
Ibizan bread pudding with Caleta coffee 198
Easy peasant bread from Ibiza 78
Pan con tomate 38
Squid ink bread 22
Tapa with squid ink bread 22

Cheese
Endive tapa with Cabrales cheese and walnuts 30
Grilled figs with Iberian ham and goat cheese 18
Iberian cupcakes with Manchego cheese 148
Iberian grilled sandwich 142
Manchego cheese marinated in olive oil 32
Pan con tomate with Manchego cheese 38
Vegetarian croquettes 28

Chocolate
Braised Oxtail in a red wine-chocolate sauce 90
Bread with chocolate, olive oil and salt 192
Churros with a spicy chocolate sauce 194
Creamy mashed cauliflower with white chocolate and vanilla 158

Chorizo
Breaded chicken rolls with saffron mayonnaise 92
Chorizo croutons with grapes and Iberian pork secreto 76
Chorizo-mango-tonic-jelly 170
Crunchy chickpeas with spinach 132
Garlic soup 58
Iberian cupcakes with chorizo 148
Lentil soup with shrimp and chorizo skewers 56
Lentil soup with chorizo crumble 56
Scallops with chorizo 160
Tapa with squid ink bread 22

Dates
Stuffed dates and Serrano ham pinchos 18

Drinks (sangria, Gin-Tonic and Spanish wines)
Cava Sangria with Vodka for beginners 208
Spanish Gin and Tonic 210
Spanish wines 212
White sangria for 'the advanced' 208

Fish, crustaceans and shellfish
Basque fish soup 50
Cod confit 152
Cod with aioli au gratin 151
Crunchy chickpeas with spinach 132
Galician style Scallops 160
Tuna empanada from Galicia 96
Marinated mussels 106
Mussels in salsa brava 106
Mussels with a saffron cream sauce 106
Salted cod fritters 24
Scallops with chorizo 160
Seabass baked in herbed salt crust 102
Seafood salad 120
Spanish fish stew 100

Iberian and/or Serrano ham
Banana and Serrano ham pinchos 18
Breaded chicken rolls with saffron mayonnaise 92
Grilled figs with Iberian ham and goat cheese 18
Iberian or Serrano ham croquettes 26
Iberian grilled sandwich 142
Iberian salad with caramelized melon 118
Pan con tomate with Serrano or Iberian ham 38
Stuffed dates and Serrano ham pinchos 18

Lentils
Vegetarian lentil soup 56

Meat and poultry
Braised Oxtail in a red wine-chocolate sauce 90
Breaded chicken rolls with saffron mayonnaise 92
Cabbage rolls with Iberian sausage 84
Chorizo croutons with grapes and Iberian pork secreto 76
Paella from Valencia 82
Potato-meatball Barceloneta style 20
Roast leg of lamb Segovian style 88
Spanish meatballs with a silky tomato-saffron sauce 86

Melon
Grilled watermelon with tomato salad 116
Iberian salad with caramelized melon 118

Mushrooms
Mushroom pinchos 18
Vegetarian bean stew 52
Vegetarian paella 136

Octopus and Squid
Black rice 154
Galician style octopus 156
Grilled octopus 158
Stuffed squid in ink sauce 110
Spanish fish stew 100
Squid ink bread 22
Squid ink bun with calamari 140
Tapa with squid ink bread 22

Olives
Almond-olive spread 45
Marinated olives with lemon, garlic and fennel 44
Olive spread 45

Padrón pepers
Fried Padron peppers 70

Potatoes
Cod with aioli au gratin 151
Creamy mashed potatoes 158
Creamy purple mashed potatoes 158
Creamy saffron mashed potatoes 158
Fried potato cubes with a spicy sauce 68
Potato-meatball Barceloneta style 20
Potato aioli 152
Scrumptious fried eggs 66
Spanish potato omelet 64
Roast leg of lamb Segovian style 88
Vegetarian Russian potato salad 72

Rice
Black rice 154
Creamy rice pudding from Asturias 188
Paella from Valencia 82
Vegetarian blood sausage 134
Vegetarian paella 136

Saffron
Breaded chicken rolls with saffron mayonnaise 92
Cod Confit 152
Cod with aioli au gratin 151
Creamy saffron mashed potatoes 158
Mussels with a saffron cream sauce 106
Paella from Valencia 82
Saffron crema catalana 200
Spanish fish stew 100
Spanish meatballs with a silky tomato-saffron sauce 86
Vegetarian paella 136

Shrimp
Basque fish soup 50
Garlic Shrimp 104
Grilled shrimp 98
Lentil soup with chorizo and shrimp skewers 56
Mushroom pinchos 18
Shrimp croquettes 28
Spanish fish stew 100

Sweets (desserts, cakes, pies)
Almond cake from Santiago 186
Aniseed cookies 204
Bread with chocolate, olive oil and salt 192
Catalonian All Saints' Day cookies 184
Churros with a spicy chocolate sauce 194
Creamy rice pudding from Asturias 188
Ibizan bread pudding with Caleta coffee 198
Ibizan cheesecake 202
Mini butter cakes from Astorga 190
Saffron crema catalana 200
Spanish (French) toast 181

Tomato
Creamy, silky gazpacho 54
Grilled watermelon with tomato salad 116
Iberian salad with caramelized melon 118
Pan con tomate 38
Pan con tomate with Manchego cheese 38
Pan con tomate with Serrano or Iberian ham 38
Pan con tomate, vegetarian version 38
Romesco sauce 176
Spanish meatballs with a silky tomato-saffron sauce 86
Tomato jam 45

Vegetables
Cabbage rolls with Iberian sausage 84
Caramelized leeks with romesco sauce 130
Cauliflower aioli 152
Creamy mashed cauliflower with white chocolate and vanilla 158
Creamy, silky gazpacho 54
Crunchy chickpeas with spinach 132
Eggplant chips with honey 34
Endive tapa with Cabrales cheese and walnuts 30
Green Pea pancakes 144
Grilled asparagus 122
Ibiza-style pizza with grilled vegetables 74
Roasted vegetable salad 124
Smoky bean salad 128
Vegetarian bean stew 52
Vegetarian lentil soup 56
Vegetarian paella 136
Vegetarian Russian potato salad 72
Winter salad with blood orange 114

Vegetarian
Almond-olive spread 45
Almond gazpacho 48
Blackberry mayonnaise 45
Caramelized leeks with romesco sauce 130
Chorizo croutons with grapes and Iberian pork secreto (vegetarian variation) 76
Creamy mashed cauliflower with white chocolate and vanilla 158
Creamy mashed potatoes 158
Creamy purple mashed potatoes 158
Creamy saffron mashed potatoes 158
Creamy, silky gazpacho 54
Crunchy chickpeas with spinach (vegetarian variation) 132
Eggplant chips with honey 34
Endive tapa with Cabrales cheese and walnuts 30
Fried potato cubes with a spicy sauce 68
Green Pea pancakes 144
Garlic soup (vegetarian variation) 58
Grilled asparagus 122
Grilled watermelon with tomato salad 116
Ibiza-style pizza with grilled vegetables 74
Marinated olives with lemon, garlic and fennel 44
Pan con tomate 38
Pan con tomate with Manchego 38
Pan con tomate, vegetarian version 38
Roasted vegetable salad 124
Scrumptious fried eggs 66
Smoky bean salad 128
Spanish omelet 64
Squid ink bread (vegetarian variation) 22
Squid ink bun with calamari (vegetarian variation) 140
Tapa with squid ink bread (vegetarian variation) 22
Toasted bread with vegan sobrasada, honey and almonds 44
Tomato jam 45
Tuna empanada from Galicia (vegetarian variation) 96
Vegan chorizo spread 44
Vegetarian bean stew 52
Vegetarian blood sausage 134
Vegetarian croquettes 28
Vegetarian lentil soup 56
Vegetarian paella 136
Vegetarian Russian potato salad 72
Winter salad with blood orange 114

Sponsors
Sligro Haarlem (food and tableware)- www.sligro.com
Valderrama (olive oil) –www.valderrama.nl
Dennis Diem (clothes Sandra)- www.dennisdiem.nl
Cavallaro Napoli (clothes Daniel and Rueben)- www.cavallaro.nl

Bamix- www.bamix.nl
Berry van Galen (cooking video's www.sandraskitchen.nl)-www.mediaopmaat.nl
Dille & Kamille (tableware)-www.dille-kamille.nl
Nga Ho Styling (shoes and jewelry Sandra)
Witloft (aprons)-www.wit-loft.com

Locations
House Paco and Michela Diaz, Can Furnet, Ibiza
House Lola Pop Brood, Santa Gertudis, Ibiza - www.lolapopbrood.com
Ibiza Horses – www.ibizahorses.es
Supermarket El rincón de escodolar, Ibiza - facebook.com/elrincondeescodolar/
Restaurante Mar a vila, Ibiza - www.maravilaibiza.es
Restaurante La Escollera, Ibiza www.laescolleraibiza.com
Ecoshop Finca Ecológica, Ibiza
 facebook.com/Ecoshop-Finca-ecologica-Ibiza-794398860606573/
Mercado La Boquería, Barcelona

Spanish Tourist Office, The Hague, The Netherlands -www.spain.info/nl/tourspain
Embassy of Spain, The Hague, The Netherlands –www.rijksoverheid.nl

¡Gracias!
— Acknowledgements!

I would like to thank the following wonderful people who have helped me realize my dream.

Daniel, my husband and my official taster, for your support and indispensable feedback and for being such a willing and enthusiastic customer. For being willing to eat only Spanish food for months on end and not complaining about gaining a few extra pounds in the process.

Andrea, my daughter, for all the time and energy you put into this book. For your wonderfully inspiring ideas and food styling. For always being prepared to help me and encourage me whenever I got stuck and could not face another Spanish dish.

Rueben, my son, another willing and enthusiastic customer, for coming to the house so many times to test all of the dishes. You helped me so much with your honest critiques. No food critic can compete!

My Spanish relatives and Julia, my mother, who instilled in me the love for Spanish food and all my loved ones for whom I love to cook.

Carin Verbruggen & Ferry Drenthem Soesman, for the magnificent photography and layout, the unforgettable photo shoots in Amsterdam, Ibiza and Barcelona. For your endless patience and your friendship.

Liesbeth Ribbink, my dear friend, who translated ¡Sabor Sabor! into English with heart and soul. With an unfailing eye and indispensable feedback. Bravo!

Dennis Diem, for your friendship and the beautiful dresses, in particular the red one you designed especially for me.

Giuseppe Cavallaro, for the elegant clothing with a Mediterranean touch. I love a man in a great suit.

Sligro Haarlem, for your enthusiasm and your interest, for sponsoring the food and non-food items for this book. I always feel welcome in your store.

Michiel van der Eerde and Robert Kranenborg, my mentors during MasterChef Holland. Michiel for writing the preface for this book and Robert for his wise and touching words. Thank you both for your confidence in me. You have taught me to seek harmony in my cooking, honoring each ingredient's integrity and not making too much of a mess in the kitchen.

Jessica Durlacher, for your friendship and all the years of cooking together. I was honored that you were willing to write a few beautiful and kind words in my book.

Barbara Luijken, my editor, for your heroism and for your endless patience while creating order in my chaos.

Terra Lannoo publishing, who gave me the chance to realize my dream; along with Yvonne Twisk and Paul Römer, my publishers, who believed in me and had the courage to embark on this adventure.

© 2019
Uitgeverij TERRA
Terra is part of Uitgeverij TerraLannoo bv
P.O. Box 23202
1100 DS Amsterdam, The Netherlands
info@terralannoo.nl
www.terra-publishing.com

Text and concept: Sandra Alvarez Chin Sue
Translation: Liesbeth Ribbink
Photography: Carin Verbruggen & Ferry Drenthem Soesman
Design: Studio Carin Verbruggen & Ferry Drenthem Soesman
Design Cover: hans delnoij grafisch ontwerp, Overpelt (B)
Foodstyling: Andrea Alvarez
Editors: Barbara Luijken, Marijke Overpelt
Editors for English: Textcase, The Netherlands
Typesetting: Rogier Stoel, The Netherlands

ISBN: 978 90 8989 800 5
NUR: 442

All rights reserved. No part of this publication may be reproduced, stored in a retrieval system or transmitted in any form by any means, electronic, mechanical, photocopying, recording or otherwise without the prior permission of the publisher.